THE NAUGHTY
BUT NICE
REVOLUTION

THE NAUGHTY BUT NICE REVOLUTION

How thousands of owners of
barking, lunging, reactive dogs are
transforming their stuggles
through games and SO CAN YOU

A PRACTICAL GUIDE

TOM MITCHELL and LAUREN LANGMAN

The Choir Press

First published in the United Kingdom in 2020 by

The Choir Press

ISBN 978-1-78963-091-6

DEDICATION

Tom: This is dedicated to all the Night Walkers, to those who have tried to make life better for a Naughty But Nice dog.

It's to the owners who have been told time and time again that there is no hope (and refuse to believe the naysayers!). You are heroes. Your dog could not ask for a better owner.

Lauren: To Popi, the original Naughty But Nice dog, who took me from a Night Walker to a Gamechanger. Dog, companion, spirit guide: you took me on a journey I didn't know I needed to go on, and what a journey it was! Thank you for showing me the way. Shine bright, darling girl.

ACKNOWLEDGEMENTS

With love and thanks to our dogs, families, friends, team and tribe. Gamechanges all. We couldn't do it without you.

CONTENTS

INTRODUCTION

Life with a naughty dog can be tough.

It gets you down. It wreaks havoc with your home life. It cripples your self-confidence and hugely challenges the bond you have with your dog. It crushes your dog ownership dreams of long countryside walks and a quiet pub lunch with your dog. It can be dangerous – for you, your family, your dog, and other humans and dogs your dog meets.

It is a tiring way to live. Every move has to be considered, every plan carefully detailed to take account of your dog's needs. There is no spontaneity and there is absolutely zero prospect of it being relaxing. It is exhausting.

Then comes the guilt. Does your dog hate you? Is it something you did wrong? Did you miss a sign or omit to teach them something vital? Have you failed them?

And then comes the saddest:

Am I the best owner for my dog?

Is my dog crazy? Is there something wrong with them? Are they aggressive or particularly mean spirited? Are they vicious? Are they dangerous?

Which leads to:

Is this the best home for my dog?

And the ultimate:

Are my dog's issues incompatible with life?

Naughty But Nice dog ownership can be a brutally lonely, sad and confusing place. The questions you find yourself asking are truly terrifying and certainly not what most owners have in mind when they bring their new family member home. There's a sadness that comes with the realisation that the life you had planned for your puppy or new rescue dog is not going to be the one you envisaged.

But…

There is another way.

What if we told you that your Naughty But Nice struggles can be turned into strengths?

That no dog or owner is ever lost?

And that changing your situation doesn't have to be hard or compli-cated – that it will even be *fun*?

Welcome to the Gamechanger way.

Facing the fear

First, we would like to clear up one thing – the most common fear of Naughty But Nice dog owners: the fear that you are not the right owner for your dog.

Please be assured that you are *absolutely* the *right* owner for your dog.

That is so important that it bears repeating: You are absolutely the right owner for your dog.

More than that, your dog is lucky to have you. Because if you have taken the time to notice your dog's behaviour and considered questions like those above, and have taken steps to help your dog such as attending training classes, watching training videos, taking courses and reading up on it (as indicated by the fact you are holding this book) – if you *care* enough to try to help your dog, then you are absolutely, 100%, the right owner for your dog.

Do you realise how lucky your dog is to have you? Many dog owners don't even notice that their dog has an issue. Your dog really landed on their paws when you walked into their life!

A caveat

Not every dog is right for every home and sometimes the very best thing you can do for them is to realise and accept that. If the very best thing for your dog is that they would be better suited to living in another home, then make those arrangements with love and care and know that you are doing the very best you can by your dog. It is a brave, selfless act and there is no shame in putting your dog's needs first.

We are however super confident that the majority of issues can be resolved by following the Gamechanger way that you will find in this book so don't despair. Read on!

So you have a Naughty But Nice dog – what next?

Accept that the life you had planned with your dog has changed

Life with your Naughty But Nice dog isn't going to be what you'd planned. But it can, and will, be awesome. Your Naughty But Nice dog might never sit quietly beside you in the pub while you enjoy lunch, but they will take you on a journey of discovery unlike any other. You'll learn lessons that you would not have learned had your dog been 'normal'. You'll create a bond so unique with your dog that it will light up both your world and your dog's. You'll find a new way of living and training that will change both your lives forever.

Know that there is something you can do about it

When you are living and coping with a Naughty But Nice dog, it can be hard to see any light at the end of the tunnel. Everything feels so rigid, so difficult and so set in stone. But please know that your dog is so, so changeable and you are so, so changeable, and your situation is so, so changeable. And the amazing news? The power to change everything lies in your hands.

Know that this is your unique path and it is way better than you could ever have imagined

Your Naughty But Nice dog has come into your life to show you a better way than you could ever have imagined. The path of the 'normal' dog life? That is not for you. Let it go. The path you and your dog will walk together is so unique, so wonderful that one day you will look back and give thanks for the long overcome issues that set you off on that road.

Our mission

Our mission is to bring those who feel alone, trapped, struggling, overwhelmed by their issues with their Naughty But Nice issues into the light, to bring them home into our Naughty But Nice fold and show them that there is hope. We are talking about those who have ever been excluded from a training class or maybe have never even made it to a training class because their dog's issues are too severe, who have had to quit a dog sport because their dog couldn't cope, who have had to live with strict rules separating their dog and visitors because of behavioural issues, who walk at night to avoid others, who live in fear of the postie losing a finger, who have perhaps been bitten themselves by their dogs, who feel their relationship with their dog is irreparably broken, who feel that there is no way forward – this book is for you.

This book – and all of our transformational online dog training solutions – are a safe place for such owners and their dogs, where issues can be laid bare and fully addressed, where you can speak without fear of judgement and learn without shame about the position you find yourself in. Lay down your lonely burden and let us show you the Gamechanger way. You have found your tribe. You are home.

The origins of Naughty But Nice

Lauren's story:

Naughty But Nice came about because of a very special dog: Popi. Popi is my 16-year-old border collie and she was a handful when she was a youngster. She would growl and lunge at other dogs so I took her to training. Any time she grumbled at another dog the trainer threw a chain at the back of her legs. I was horrified, but being naive and inexperienced I thought this was just the way things had to be to address the issues. I thought that it would lead her to a happier and better life in the long term. I've lived with the guilt of that ever since.

And what happened? Did the chain work? Did Popi realise the error of her ways and stop growling? No. She stopped growling, but went straight to biting. As she was getting punished for giving a warning, she went straight to the point.

I hated what I had allowed to be done to her. I hated the outcome. I hated the damage it had caused her and our relationship. I hated how I felt about it. I wanted to learn a better way for Popi, and as I learned more I wanted to share that way with others, with those in the same position that we had been in. I knew there had to be a better way. I structured my own classes carefully so that dogs with issues could attend without fear. I welcomed those who other trainers and training classes had turned away.

And so Naughty But Nice was born. It grew firstly into its own specific group, then into short training camps, then into a week-long training camp, then developed online. It is now a worldwide movement. The Naughty But Nice tribe reaches around the globe. I am so proud and so glad that we can help those who need it anywhere in the world. I never want anyone to feel the way I did when that trainer hit my beloved dog with a chain.

The Gamechanger way

Those who train with us truly are Gamechangers. They are creative, innovative, flexible, optimistic, fun loving, resourceful and effective. They get real-life results every day. They are taking the world of dog training and turning it on its head – bringing the joy, bringing the fun, always ready to turn a struggle into a strength, and always ready with a battle cry of *"there's a game for that!"*

No dog and owner is ever lost. The Gamechanger way is inclusive and life changing. It is being ready to meet issues head on and find creative ways to tackle them. It is sharing information and working together to learn and grow. It is supporting others through the tough times, celebrating their wins and shouting their successes from the rooftops. It is championing what is best for our dogs and always seeking to develop, learn and improve.

It gets real-life results.

It is awesome.

The Gamechanger Manifesto

Here's to the Gamechangers

To the owners who see struggles and turn them into strengths

The solution seekers

The owners that never accept a relationship and dog is lost

To the game players

The fun makers

The joy finders

The owners who inspire rather than force or deprive

To those who when faced with a struggle scream

'There's a game for that'

Who reach out and grab real-life results

and never (never) stop transforming through games

So here's to the Gamechangers, and here's to you, Gamechanger. We are going to take you on a journey of transformation. Are you ready to turn your Naughty But Nice struggles to strengths, to get real-life results, to live an awesome Gamechanger life? Let's begin.

CHAPTER 1

THE NIGHT-TIME WALKERS

What is a Naughty But Nice dog?

So let's dig a little deeper – what actually is a Naughty But Nice dog?

Let's start by thinking about what they look like:

- *The dog barking and lunging at the end of a lead when it sees a dog in the distance.*

- *The dog who runs off instantly the second it catches a scent and will not recall.*

- *The dog who chases cyclists or joggers.*

- *The dog who obsessively guards their toys or food.*

- *The dog who cries when you leave the house.*

- *The dog who tries to hump you every time you sit down.*

These are just some examples. The list of Naughty But Nice issues is endless. You know you have a Naughty But Nice issue if your dog is behaving in a way that impacts on your normal daily living experience. For example, occasionally pulling on lead because your dog is excited to be approaching the park is normal – pulling you so hard whenever the lead is on that you cannot walk your dog is a problem. It is subjective and particular to you and your situation with your dog.

A short note

If your dog starts exhibiting Naughty But Nice behaviours, you should check with your vet that there is no physical reason for the behavioural change. Pain can change the behaviour of even the mildest mannered dog. Keep an eye on what is normal for your dog and if anything changes – from odd to outrageous – get it checked out.

Hallmarks of the Naughty But Nice owner

If you have a Naughty But Nice dog, there is a good chance you are a Night-Time Walker. Night-Time Walkers are a less frequently spotted type of dog owner, rarely seen by the general public. And that is exactly as they want it. Their dogs have issues so serious that walking during daytime hours, when you might meet other members of the public and their dogs, just isn't an option. The cover of darkness is the Night-Time Walker's friend and they will wait until after dark or get up before the sun rises to walk their dogs in that time of solitude.

Night-Time Walkers are so keen to avoid contact with anything that will trigger their dog's difficult behaviour that they will go to any lengths to avoid others, even putting themselves in dangerous situations by walking at anti-social hours, in isolated areas. The benefit is that they are unlikely to meet anyone that will trigger their dog. The drawback is that there isn't anyone around to help should anything go awry. It is lonely and sometimes dangerous practice.

But Night-Time Walkers don't just roam around the streets at midnight. They sit in the corners of training classes, eyeing the exits. They watch others participate in dog sports, desperately wishing they could take part. They sleep in their vans at dog sport events because their dogs can't cope with being in hotels. They just long for a 'normal' dog and a 'normal' life.

Living with a Naughty But Nice dog

Life with a Naughty But Nice dog can be hard. Just navigating the day with Naughty But Nice issues to consider can be exhausting. There can be many practical considerations that have to be taken into account, for example, your dog requiring to be muzzled at certain times or in certain circumstances, arranging life in a 'gated community' so that your dog does not encounter the cat, having to restrict visitors to your home, having to keep the floor clear so your dog will not chew items, the list goes on and on.

There is also a significant emotional toll in living with a Naughty But Nice dog.

WHAT DIFFICULT BEHAVIOURS DOES YOUR DOG EXHIBIT?

DIFFICULT BEHAVIOURS

MY DOG

THEY MAKE ME FEEL...

A Naughty but Nice Dog can make you feel:

- Embarrassed
- Shame
- Not capable
- Worried
- Anxious
- Out of your depth
- Stressed
- Lacking confidence
- Conflicted
- Not wanting to participate
- Restricted
- Upset
- Excluded
- Frightened
- Apprehensive about what life holds for you both.

You can feel like you've let your dog down, like you've let yourself down, like you've let your family down. You can feel worthless, embarrassed, guilty and stupid. You can berate yourself for not having done enough or for having done the wrong thing by your dog. You can feel massively disempowered and like you simply don't know what to do.

If your dog is not behaving in a way that is socially acceptable, it changes everything. Doors don't just close on you; they get slammed shut. The dreams you had for your dog ownership evaporate. People just don't understand. It is painful.

HOW OWNING A NAUGHTY BUT NICE DOG CAN MAKE YOU FEEL

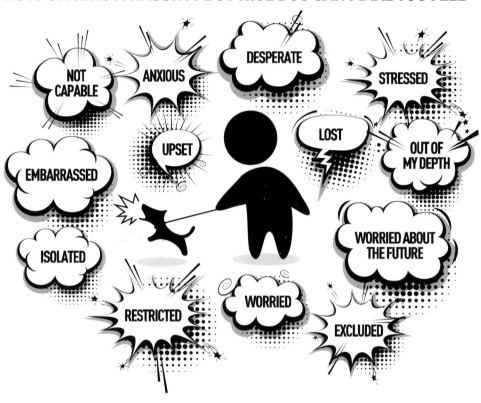

A change of approach

The problem is that we misinterpret the dog's behaviour as problem behaviour because of the impact it has. Ultimately, however, it is just dog behaviour. It is your dog's way of expressing that all is not well with them or in their world. They can't cope with something that life is throwing at them and they are simply telling you that. They don't hate you. They don't hate other dogs. They are not trying to dominate you or take over the house. They have not declared war on cyclists. There is simply something about the situation that their brain is unable to deal with.

The difficulty is that we judge the dog's behaviour rather than trying to understand what is behind it. In our desperation to stop the behaviour, we treat the symptom rather than the cause. Barking, lunging, chasing, whining, biting, pulling on lead, failing to recall, all pose difficulties for going about our daily lives and we just want the dog to stop. We want them to behave in ways we see as appropriate but they are unable to do so. The problem is that we often attempt to implement a solution that is more of a sticking plaster than a cure because the issues with the dog's coping mechanisms remain undiscovered and unresolved.

Seeking help

Naughty But Nice owners have often attended many different training sessions or sought assistance from behaviourists or vets. They have often spent a lot of money, and possibly even gone to extreme lengths in terms of lifestyle change or training practices in an attempt to resolve their dog's issues.

The emotional and physical impacts of owning a Naughty But Nice dog and the overwhelming desire to resolve the situation can lead Naughty But Nice owners to try anything. Like Lauren with Popi back in the day, we place ourselves in the hands of people who appear to know better, those with the answers who will help us resolve this distressing situation. It leaves us vulnerable, not just to the charlatans who have no idea how to resolve such profound issues, but also to those who are well meaning and may be able to get results, but not in the best possible way and not with the best possible practices for long-term change.

If you're that Naughty But Nice owner, please know that we appreciate that you may have had bad experiences. You may have tried so hard and spent so much money, all for nothing. We understand how frustrating that is. It is good to remain critical. You should always apply your mind to what you are being told. But rest assured, you have found your home. You are going to remember this time as the catalyst for change in your life with your dog. You have made the best decision and you are now in the place of real-life results.

Why couldn't previous trainers 'fix' my Naughty But Nice dog?

Surely there are only so many ways to train a dog? Dog training is dog training, right? Not so. As dog training has evolved, three typical types of trainer have emerged.

The three types of trainer

TRAINER ONE

Trainer Ones get results by using force and intimidation. They will use tools such as choke chains, prong collars, shock collars, training discs, noise bottles, rattles, sprays, etc., to force the dog to comply.

Or they may tell you to:

- Raise your voice to your dog

- Use harsh words or a harsh tone

- "Show your dog who is boss"

- Hold your dog in position, growl at them

- Make your dog do what they are told

- Try to dominate your dog.

They try to force and intimidate, and what we see happen is that relationships get damaged and the dog's behaviour gets worse.

There is a good chance that your Naughty But Nice dog is afraid of certain situations. When you start behaving in an unpredictable, scary, aggressive manner, your dog is unlikely to be able to cope and their behaviour is likely to worsen. And if you add pain into the mix, by introducing shock or prong collars, for example, the results can be detrimental to your dog's mental health and well-being, their behaviour, and the relationship you have with your dog.

TRAINER TWO

Trainer Two types train dogs using reward-based training methods.

What might that look like?

- They use food.

- They use toys.

- They talk about reward-based training.

- They teach specific behaviours such as sit, down, stand, loose lead walking

That's not a bad thing – the Gamechanger way uses positive, reward-based training. However, the problem is that Trainer Two type training focuses on behaviours. Trainer Twos are constantly telling the dog what to do. They rely on managing the situation. The dog is not taught to think for themselves.

Trainer Twos will train sit, down, recall and walking nicely on a loose lead, but as soon as the dog goes outside the training environment, it all falls apart. The learning just doesn't translate to real life.

With Trainer Two type training, you will learn to manage your Naughty But Nice dog's behaviour, but the behaviour itself won't be resolved and you are unlikely to get consistent results out of the training environment or in the absence of a tasty treat or toy.

TRAINER THREE

Trainer Threes play concept games. They get real-life results because they reshape the dog's brain. They arm the dog with the tools to cope with the world. And they have fun while doing it.

Teaching concepts such as impulse control, management of arousal, focus, optimism, calmness, and boundaries, as opposed to behaviours such as sit, down and stay, reshapes the dog's brain, teaches the dog to think and gives them a toolkit for dealing with any situation. That enables them to make good choices. With the concepts they learn, they can cope with any situation life throws at them. And that extinguishes the 'problem' behaviours.

Games shape the Naughty But Nice dog's brain so that the dog is able to cope with the stimulus or situation that previously overwhelmed them because their brain simply wasn't shaped to deal with it. The 'problem' behaviour is eliminated because the dog's brain is now shaped to cope with the situation.

Taught behaviours can be useful, but the reason a Trainer Three trained dog does them is not because of the way the behaviour was taught. It is down to the concepts that underlie it: self-control, focus, optimism, grit. And that is all trained through games.

Positive, not permissive

Approaching training from a fun, games-based perspective does not mean you simply become permissive. Allowing your dog to do what they like, with no boundaries and no consequences for their behaviour, is not good for your dog. Boundary-free living is a terrible responsibility to put on a dog!

Games-based concept training sets up a choice framework that will enable your dog to make good choices. It creates a framework of exposure that will guide your dog's learning to make sure that your dog learns the things that will shape their brain appropriately to address the issues that need to be addressed. It puts boundaries in place so your dog gets feedback on what is ok and what isn't. It is a method of training that will enable your dog to feel secure, thus building their confidence in their knowledge of the world and their own skills, and their ability to cope. You are setting your dog up for success, not simply allowing them to do whatever they like!

Reshaping your dog's brain

The reasons that your previous training may not have worked for you lie in the fact that Trainer One and Two type training does not address the way your dog's brain is shaped, and that shaping causes the 'problem' behaviour. Your dog's responses might be managed or you might be taught how to manage the situation, but if you don't address the reason why your dog can't cope with what is happening, then your training efforts are ultimately doomed to failure.

Trainers One and Two believe that the way to improve the problem is to work within the problem itself. They will recreate a distressing or sometimes dangerous situation that your dog has already proved unable to cope with and will try to work within it to resolve it. Trainer One does this by using force or intimidation to stop the resulting behaviour. Trainer Two attempts to create the desired behaviour in the situation.

Trainer Three recognises that your dog is in a situation where their brain cannot make the right choices. The right choice is simply not an option for your dog in that situation, so it is impossible to fix the problem while in that situation. If your dog had the option to handle that situation correctly, they would. Their brain is simply not shaped to cope with the situation. The training you do to resolve that therefore has to take place outside of the problematic situation.

It is a very human approach to problem solving to attempt to fix the problem from within it. You get into the problem, and you find a way

HOW DIFFERENT TRAINING METHODS APPROACH LEARNING

TRAINER 3
Focuses on building concepts to make
any future learning of behaviours easy.
Training for the situation, not in the situation

BRAIN

TRAINER 1
Focuses on BEHAVIOUR
and punishing unwanted
behaviour to increase
desired behaviour

TRAINER 2
Focuses on the behaviour
displayed and rewarding
that desired behaviour
IN the situation

to resolve it. But that doesn't work for your dog or the way their brain works. You need to arm your dog with the ability to cope with the situation in advance.

We often have Naughty But Nice dog owners come to us who have consulted various types of dog professionals, such as trainers, behaviourists and vets, in an attempt to resolve their dog's issues. They may have spent considerable sums of money to access help and tried many different methods, all without success. It is unfortunately not an uncommon situation.

Here's a typical example with a dog who is exhibiting reactivity towards other dogs. The owner consults a trainer, a behaviourist and a vet.

The trainer, a Trainer Two type, suggests that the dog needs to see six different types of dogs per day and is rewarded and praised for calm behaviour. The owner finds it a bit of a challenge to find six different types of dogs every day and rearranges her life around trying to source the different dogs her dog 'needs' to experience. The dog experiences a constant barrage of dogs it is unable to process encountering, but it does occasionally get a piece of sausage if he can hold it together long enough. Most of the time though, he can't.

The owner returns to the trainer, who says that she isn't doing enough and the dog will need to meet ten different dogs every day. The owner is wracked with guilt and attempts to find even more dogs. The dog meets even more dogs he can't cope with.

The behaviourist advises that that is just the way he is, so the owner should get used to it. The owner is desperately sad. Her dreams of long, relaxed walks with her dog crumble to dust. She starts walking her dog at midnight. The dog wonders why they never see daylight together.

The vet recommends medication. The owner is broken hearted but agrees to do whatever the vet thinks is necessary to help her dog live a good life. Her dog's behaviour becomes a bit flat and his tail doesn't wag as it once did, but at least he no longer cracks up at other dogs. The dog doesn't seem to feel much of anything anymore.

This example is based on real-life advice given in one of Tom's behaviour cases. It is a good example of how different professionals approach the problem. The common theme is that they will all seek to work *in* the problem, rather than *for* the problem. And that is why they don't get real-life results. Games-based concept training is the answer!

Becoming a Gamechanger

Tom's story:

I realised I wanted to change dogs' lives by getting real-life results for owners (instead of results in training and nowhere else) when I encountered a dog chained up on a farm. The dog was a failed sheepdog, trained using Trainer One methods. I encountered the dog because, one day, he escaped from his chain and became worried about the sight of someone tying their shoelace in the distance. He coped with this by jumping at the person and biting numerous times, tearing off their top lip. That person was me, and, that day, I vowed to make it my mission (admittedly in my head as the lack of top lip meant I couldn't really speak!) to find a better way and show people that better way, and that better way is games.

We want to give Naughty But Nice dog owners:

1. Hope.

2. Power to say when something is right or wrong for your dog.

3. Confidence to pursue your goal and to say "that's not my path, thanks", to do the right thing by your dog.

4. Restored faith in their relationship with their dog.

Sometimes a dog comes to you because it was meant to change your life. So often we spend so much time resisting our Naughty But Nice difficulties that we can't see them for what they are: a beautiful opportunity to learn and grow. We get it – it is hard to think that way when your dog is losing their mind when there's a knock at the door, but your dog's Naughty But Nice issues really do present an amazing opportunity to get under the hood of your dog's behaviour, to experiment and to see what can resolve the issues, in a fun and positive way. Your confidence will grow as you see real-life results and your bond with your dog will deepen no end as you work through this together.

It might not feel like it, but Naughty But Nice issues really can be blessings in disguise. They are often the catalyst for change you needed in your dog training and daily living experience with your dog.

Lauren's story:

The catalyst for change in my life as a dog trainer came when I was a very young child. I trained my Gran's neighbour's dog, a border collie called Blues. I knew the traditional ways to teach dogs how to do what you wanted them to, but Blues was too special for such boring methods. He was a fun dog; he wanted to play. He would jump the fence to come and hang out with me in my gran's garden.

Even at that young age, I could see how trainable he was and how keen he was to engage with me when we had fun together. I knew that I wanted to use that to train him, not just make him do what I told him to do. I saw the joy with which he leapt the fence when I called him. He could have chosen to stay in his own garden. But I saw what I wanted and I made it happen. I encouraged him to jump that fence in a way that suggested he was invited to the best party in town. And he was! I'd save the tastiest treats I could get my hands on for him. I'd make up fun games to play for him and we would just have the best time together.

Blues changed my life. His reaction to me and his desire to spend time with me made me realise the value of joy and fun in training. Had he been a different dog, things might have turned out very differently, but as it was, he taught me many of the values that are enshrined in the Gamechanger Manifesto today. I am incredibly grateful to him for it.

You are 100% the right owner for your dog, but your dog is also 100% the right dog for you. Your dog has come to you with these issues to teach you something. Let them change your thinking, let them change your life, let them show you the way. Anything is possible.

Does games-based training work for dogs with serious issues?

Naughty But Nice includes a constellation of behaviours, with some being more difficult than others. Can games-based concept training work for even the most serious issues, such as severe separation related behaviours, obsessive behaviours, aggression and biting?

The answer is a definite yes. This isn't just something that works on mild cases or on 'easier' dogs. Many dogs who have come through our Naughty But Nice programmes have seen at least one vet or behaviourist. Some are on medication. There are dogs whose owners have been told there is no hope and that they should just accept the situation, or that the dog's issues are such that they are incompatible with continued residence in the home, or even incompatible with life. Our method of games-based concept training has worked for these dogs.

The issues our Naughty But Nice dogs face can sometimes lead us to think of them as special. We can become conditioned by the impact of their behaviour to think of it in negative terms. They are different. They are reactive. They are troubled. But labels can be so sticky and it can be difficult to move beyond them. Naughty But Nice dogs are of course special but not so special that games will not work for them. We need to reshape their brains and we need to reshape our own brains. Don't be closed off to these transformational methods. The quality of solutions we find to a problem typically stems from the quality of the questions we ask ourselves. Think – *how can we move forward?*

Define your dog by their future rather than their past. Reignite your dreams and take back your power. Embrace the Gamechanger way of life. Change your story. Change your life. Change your dog's story. Change your dog's life.

A word of warning

As transformational as the methods described in this book are, they will only work if you do. Simply reading the information is not going to change anything. You have to understand it and do the work. Complete the resources, play the games, apply what you have learned to your own dog and your dog's issues, and use the tools we give you to resolve them.

Read and enjoy, but also do. Your dog's brain is not going to be reshaped by you reading this book, but it will if you do the work.

CHAPTER 2

YOUR POWERFUL WHY

The first step to overcoming Naughty But Nice issues is finding your powerful why. This might seem obvious: you really, really, really want your dog to stop biting your visitors. But if you look beneath that, really drill down into it, you will find what it is that is motivating you to make these changes.

Consider:

- What do you want to achieve?

- Why do you want it?

These aren't other people's whys or the whys of the Should Brigade who say you should do this or you should want that for your dog. This is your life, your story. Really examine your own mind, heart and soul, and identify what it is that is driving you to make the change. This knowledge will sustain you through the process of change and will give you a home to return to if things get tough.

Be honest, and don't forget to aim high. Remember we are casting aside old labels and aiming for awesomeness. Don't settle for good enough. Aim for spectacular.

Lauren's story:

I thought that while I had Popi, I would never have another dog. I changed that thought. Now she lives harmoniously with other dogs. Since the age of three she has never lived as an only dog. We have never had a dog fight. It would have been a disservice to myself, to Popi and to the other dogs to persist with that story.

This book is dedicated to Popi. She made Naughty But Nice a thing.

YOUR POWERFUL WHY

YOUR DOG NOW...
WHAT YOU LOVE

YOUR POWERFUL WHY

HOW YOU WANT THOSE STRUGGLES TO LOOK IN THE FUTURE

YOUR DOG NOW...
WHAT YOU STRUGGLE WITH

HOW YOU WANT THIS BOOK TO HELP YOU...

DOODLE SPACE...

The vulnerability of the learner

Other people's whys are so easy to absorb. They are so freely offered when you have a Naughty But Nice dog. People are always quick with a tip or suggestion or advice when they encounter a dog with Naughty But Nice issues. Very often that advice is not in any way relevant to the dog, their owner or their particular circumstances.

Getting clear about your own powerful why will equip you to repel such advice. It will also enable you to critically evaluate any advice you have solicited from trainers, behaviourists, vets or other dog-related professionals to ensure that any methods you implement will be right for your and your dog. Having a Naughty But Nice dog can leave you vulnerable emotionally to the advice of others. Your powerful why gives you back your power. Always assess what you are told with reference to your powerful why and you won't stray far from your path.

Think:

- What feels right?

- What feels good?

- Does it fit you and your dog?

- Are you happy with it?

- Are you confident and comfortable about saying yes or no to this?

- This is your family member – what feels logical?

> ## *Lauren's story:*
>
> *When that trainer threw a chain at Popi's legs, I was so desperate for help that I lost sight of my powerful why. I just wanted to make Popi 'better'. I didn't throw the chain myself but I went against my better judgement and allowed someone else to do it.*
>
> *Why did I do that? It was never meant badly. The trainer was just doing what they thought was best with the training knowledge they had. I was feeling inadequate already and the trainer had experience. I knew that the situation made me feel uncomfortable and was not good for me or my dog, but I didn't know what to do.*
>
> *Popi needed me to learn. She needed me to learn how to be the best owner I could be. She needed me to grow, to listen to my powerful why, to know what Popi needed, to understand her and not put her in these position. No class could have taught me that. I had to find it within myself.*

Holding tight to your powerful why will give you the courage to say, this is not for me and not for my dog. It will give you the courage to look at things in a new way. It will give you the courage to speak up and to leave if things aren't right.

It will give you the courage to be socially awkward if you need to be. One of our absoluteDog puppies – a beautiful golden spaniel puppy – doesn't like being petted by strangers. Unfortunately she is so pretty and cute that she attracts them – they always want to pet her! She will try to appease them and will roll onto her back, and they are delighted and think she loves the attention, when really she is trying to make them go away. The strangers can't know that and it is therefore up to us to say no, and not to let them pet her. It is up to us to keep her safe and to avoid placing her in that position. Our powerful why is that we are doing what is best for her, not for the strangers who want to touch her, or for us in enjoying that others appreciate her cuteness.

The power of a powerful why

In addition to being a tool for framing your decisions, having a powerful why will also enable you to gauge your progress. With a powerful why, you can define what results you want and you can monitor where you are towards achieving them. Are you on target? If not, it will guide to correct your course as needed. If you are on target, awesome: you know you are getting it right. Life in congruence with your powerful why feels authentic and that is an amazing place to be.

A powerful why can also move you from an inward focus to an outward focus. An inwardly directed powerful why can become an outwardly directed powerful why and that is when change really starts to happen in the world. You go from being motivated to change things for you and your dog, to helping to change things for others. That is what happened with us.

Changing lives

Our passion for helping our own Naughty But Nice dogs became a mission to help others. We wanted to break people free from the old ways of thinking, out of the old box that Naughty But Nice dogs were often cast into (the one labelled 'no hope'). We'd seen what transformation was possible and what could be achieved with a Naughty But Nice dog and we wanted to offer the chance of that to others. We wanted to bring Naughty But Nice owners in from the cold, to bring them to a place of acceptance and friendship, to help them rediscover their power, and to send them out into the world to shine the light of their achievements and to inspire and teach others.

We have achieved that. Our Gamechangers are massively passionate about helping Naughty But Nice dogs and their owners. They don't turn dogs away. They always have an answer or can find one. They are transforming the lives of Naughty But Nice dog owners and dogs worldwide. And it all came about because our powerful why became outwardly directed and turned a passion into a mission.

Lauren's story:

One of my favourite examples of what can happen when you have an outwardly directed powerful why is a lady called Sue and her Hungarian vizsla, Lyra. Sue was having low-level difficulties with Lyra's behaviour and she consulted a trainer who told her to use the alpha roll with Lyra (forcing the dog to lie on her side and holding her there). Sue tried to implement the advice but struggled to do it. It was harrowing for both her and the dog as she literally grappled to do what the trainer had advised. It didn't work. Lyra's behaviour worsened to the point that she was growling and bearing her teeth. Sue's daughter was terrified of Lyra. She hated the dog. The whole family had a very difficult relationship with Lyra.

Sue came to absoluteDogs in despair. She really thought there was no hope. Using games-based concept training we were able to turn things right around for Lyra, Sue and the whole family. Lyra is now nearly 16 and a very much loved dog who enjoys a great relationship with every member of the family.

Things could have been very different. Lyra's behaviour could have continued to worsen. She could have bitten. She could have been rehomed or even put to sleep. The family might never have had another dog and thus have lost out of a lifetime of the joy of dog ownership. Sue's daughter might have had a lifelong fear of dogs.

As it was, Sue found us. We worked together to put Sue and Lyra on a fabulous new path. They transformed their lives. And I got a fantastic friend out of it. Sue is now a very close friend. She is godmother to my daughter, Eliza. Eliza will grow up with a wonderful godmother, and I have a fabulous friend, all because of our mission to help those with Naughty But Nice issues. It just shows – you never know where your journey is going to take you or what will happen along the way!

Our days are made of this. We have been given an incredible gift and we are able to give that incredible gift to others. The gift of transformation. The gift of a life. How many lives have transformed through that ripple effect? And you are part of that and will continue to take it forward with your dog, with every dog you have in your life, with your family members and their relationships with dogs, with those you meet, and those you help. It is incredible.

How will you share your powerful why?

Whether you are a dog trainer or a dog owner going about your daily life, your behaviour and your interaction with your dog will influence others.

THE RIPPLE EFFECT

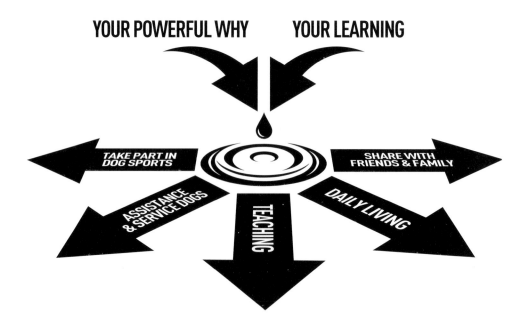

The dog trainer and the powerful why

If you are a dog trainer, you are in a direct position to influence so many dogs' lives. Let your powerful why guide you to bring the very best you can into their lives. A great trainer will do their best to move their students towards the achievement of their own individual powerful why. The outcome will be different for each person and absolutely perfect for them and their dog. Now that's incredible achievement and real-life transformation right there!

CHAPTER 3

THE NAUGHTY BUT NICE TOOLKIT

The biggest issue for owners of a Naughty But Nice dog is the feeling of disempowerment that goes with it. The feeling that you are inadequate – of not knowing what to do, of not knowing how to help your dog and how to make the behaviour stop – is painful and we are often exposed to it multiple times on a daily basis. It is crushing.

This book is going to give you back that power. It is designed to provide you with your very own Naughty But Nice toolkit. The toolkit contains a mixture of:

- **Band-Aids:** games and tools that will get you out of a situation until you can work on it (thus preventing the problem from getting worse)

- **Knowledge:** knowing when to get your dog out of a situation or use your tools to manage it

- **Cures:** games that are going to work on the issues underlying your dog's Naughty But Nice behaviour

- **Inner power:** learning to rely on the power within you and not depend on external tools.

Your Naughty But Nice toolkit will give you everything you need to handle your dog's Naughty But Nice issues in the short term, and work on the issues that underlie them in the long term with a view to eradicating the behaviours completely.

Having the Naughty But Nice toolkit will make y
you back the feeling of being in control of your _
that is so often lost when you are living with a Naug_.
You don't need to use all of the tools, but you know t.
you need them. It is a very reassuring place to be.

Practical toolkit for Naughty But Nice success

Feeling physically prepared can really lower your stress levels when handling your Naughty But Nice dog. Leaving the house in a rush and having forgotten key items does not put anyone in a great mindset, and your dog will feel it.

Here's our go-to practical toolkit for heading out and about:

1. A variety of food – lots of different types of food, in different sizes (small pieces to bigger chunks). Always pay lowest value first. If you start high, you have nowhere to go!

2. Leads and long lines, double leads, single leads.

3. Harness, head collars.

4. Somewhere for your dog to chill if you need to leave them. Use your vehicle like a mobile home from home. A covered crate in your car makes an excellent portable bedroom for your dog. Be careful of where you park – for instance, at events, don't park next to a vehicle with barking dogs in it or park on a busy thoroughfare or in direct sight of a working ring. Think of anything in the surroundings that might be disturbing to your dog, and move if necessary. If your dog is visiting or coming into a venue with you, take a portable boundary such as a travel crate, raised bed or mat to give your dog somewhere they can go to relax and enjoy a bit of space.

Camera and tripod (it doesn't have to be expensive!) so you can take videos of your training.

6. Any props needed for conversation starters or other games your dog loves, for example, target stick or block.

7. Water and a travel bowl: dehydrated dogs make bad decisions (like people).

8. Muzzle/cone as needed. All dogs should be trained to wear a muzzle. You never know when your dog might need to wear one, for example, if they require emergency vet treatment and are struggling due to pain, it is not the right time to introduce a muzzle for the first time! Muzzles are also sometimes required for public transport. They can prove handy in a variety of situations, so it pays to have your dog used to them beforehand.

9. Clicker.

10. Mobile phone.

11. Poop bags. Don't forget your poop bags. Getting caught short of poop bags is not a great situation for any dog owner, never mind having a dog whose Naughty But Nice issues render it impossible to approach another dog owner to ask if they have any spares!

TOP TIP

If you find opening poop bags tricky and feel your anxiety rising in that moment when you are wrestling with all your might with the plastic in an attempt to work it open and not thus able to fully attend to what your dog is doing and experiencing, pre-open your poop bags before you leave the house.

YOUR PRACTICAL NAUGHTY BUT NICE TOOLKIT CHECKLIST

NAUGHTY BUT NICE TOOLKIT CHECKLIST

- ☐ A VARIETY OF FOOD
- ☐ LEADS AND LONG LINES, DOUBLE LEADS, SINGLE LEADS.
- ☐ HARNESS, HEAD COLLARS.
- ☐ SOMEWHERE FOR YOUR DOG TO CHILL IF YOU NEED TO LEAVE THEM.
- ☐ CAMERA AND CHEAP TRIPOD SO YOU CAN TAKE VIDEOS OF YOUR TRAINING.
- ☐ ANY PROPS NEEDED FOR CONVERSATION STARTERS OR OTHER GAMES YOUR DOG LOVES, FOR EXAMPLE, TARGET STICK, BLOCK.
- ☐ WATER AND A TRAVEL BOWL: DEHYDRATED DOGS MAKE BAD DECISIONS (LIKE PEOPLE).
- ☐ CLICKER
- ☐ MOBILE PHONE
- ☐ POOP BAGS
- ☐ MUZZLE/CONE AS NEEDED.

- ☐ _____
- ☐ _____
- ☐ _____
- ☐ _____
- ☐ _____
- ☐ _____
- ☐ _____

Preparation is key. It allows you to feel like you've got it – and once you've got it, you are going to be unstoppable. You are making a difference to your life and your dog's life. It is enabling. It is empowering. It is inspiring. Get prepared and get going. Go you!

The tools

In addition to your starter practical toolkit, you will also need some tools to get you started in your Naughty But Nice work. Pack these items and you will never be stuck when Naughty But Nice situations arise:

1. Intuition

2. Games

3. Calmness

4. Conversation starters

5. Honesty

6. Acceptance

7. Confidence

Intuition

Trust your gut instinct – if something feels wrong, don't do it. Class situations, walks, whatever – if something doesn't feel right for you or your dog, don't do it or get out of there. All too often we bow to the external pressure of society, friends and family, convention, peers, trainers. But you know what is right for you and your dog. Your gut will tell you. Take a moment to check in with how you feel and don't be frightened to stand up for what you and your dog need.

Games

You and your dog have a joint relationship bank account, and as with a financial bank account, it has a balance. The higher the balance, the better your relationship with your dog. The lower the balance, the more chance you have of experiencing difficulties.

The bad news is that life and the world conspire to make withdrawals from your relationship bank account, some of which we cannot control.

Examples of such negative interactions include:

- Vet visits

- Travelling

- Dog reacting to events or the environment

- Your dog being scared

- Use of aversive training methods or tools including choke chains, shock or prong collars, shaking bottles, water pistols, shouting at your dog

- Frustration in training

- Disappointment in your dog

These can create a negative shared experience with your dog, and that withdraws from your account. The Naughty But Nice life is typically filled with experiences that make heavy withdrawals from the relationship bank account.

Positive interactions pay into your relationship bank account and rebuild the balance depleted by the negative interactions that life and the world throw at you. So the more positive interactions you can pay into your account, the higher your balance will be and the better protected your relationship will be from those inevitable withdrawals.

Games are the ultimate positive pay-in to your relationship bank account. Nothing builds the bond between you and your dog like playing games. Know what your dog's favourite game is and be ready to play. Have a stock of games up your sleeve at all times, and always be learning new ones. Keep it fresh and exciting and play, play, play!

Calmness

Calmness is a concept that is often massively lacking in Naughty But Nice dogs. It is often completely missing in a Naughty But Nice life! Calmness is a fundamental tool for your toolkit and cultivating calmness in your dog is key to helping them deal with whatever life throws at them.

The Calmness Triad

The Calmness Triad provides an excellent framework for teaching your dog calmness.

THE CALMNESS TRIAD

PASSIVE CALMING ACTIVITIES

- Scatter Feeding
- Meaty Bones
- Filled Kongs
- Treat Balls
- Filled Tracheas
- Dehydrated Treats
- Scenting
- Puzzle Feeders

CALMNESS PROTOCOL

Feed whenever calm, time with external distractions, and if you don't want to train then pop them in a crate or give them a passive calming activity, don't get frustrated

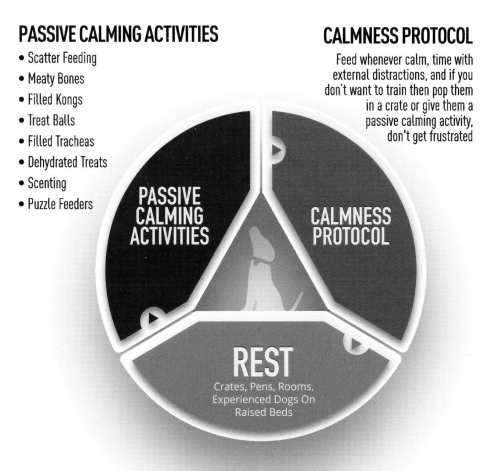

PASSIVE CALMING ACTIVITIES

CALMNESS PROTOCOL

REST
Crates, Pens, Rooms, Experienced Dogs On Raised Beds

We teach our dogs to be calm by rotating them through the Calmness Triad by:

- Working with them on their calmness protocol by feeding them when they are calm, timing feeding with external distractions and practising delivering rewards in a calm manner;

- Providing them with passive calming activities such as scatter feeding, meaty bones, filled Kongs, treat balls, scenting, dehydrated treats, filled tracheas and puzzle feeders; and

- Providing our dogs with appropriate rest in crates, pens, rooms or on raised beds.

It is not healthy for our dogs to live lives where they are permanently 'on'. Introducing the Calmness Triad to your dog's daily living will tremendously improve the quality of their life and boost their ability to cope with anything that they encounter throughout the day.

Boundary games are brilliant for taking your dog through the Calmness Triad. You work on your calmness protocol by feeding when they are calm, reward your dog generously for choosing to rest appropriately and putting a huge value on their places of rest by providing them with passive calming activities there such as scatter feeding.

Our favourite games for getting started with boundaries are Reward Nothing and Love that Boundary.

Reward Nothing

In this game, you are rewarding your dog for not reacti
from your dog's daily allowance, feed promptly but
anything occurs that would usually trigger an overexcite⏗   ⏗se
from your dog.

The key here is to get in quickly with the food before they begin
reacting. You have to reward while they are still calm. Waggling a
piece of food in front of your dog's face while they are reacting in an
attempt to distract them is not the same thing! Get in quickly and
feed them while they are doing nothing. The aim is to develop a reaction that when something exciting happens, your dog remains calm
and turns to check in with you.

Start easy by playing this in the home with minimal, low-level triggers. Then work up to more challenging triggers, and build up to
taking it on tour to the outside world.

Love That Boundary

Boundary games involve your dog staying within a defined area (e.g.
a dog bed) calmly until released – how nice would that be! These
games keep the world protected from your dog and your dog
protected from the world.

Pick an appropriate boundary – raised beds work really well for this
as it is easy for the dog to know when they are or are not on the bed.
Reward any interaction with the bed or boundary (for example
looking towards it, stepping towards it or putting a paw on it).

Allow your dog to choose to approach the bed with no verbal cue.
You want your dog to make the choice to go there.

Feed generously for being on the bed. Drip feed to the bed, rather than directly to the dog. Feed for calmness. Feed slowly.

Release your dog from the bed with a cue such as "ok" or "break". Throw food away from the bed a moment after the verbal release cue.

Then wait for your dog to choose to orient towards the bed, approach it or return to it. Don't cue the behaviour. Let your dog make the choice. When they do, reward hugely. You'll find your dog is soon popping straight back onto the bed as they know that is where the reward happens.

Once your dog values being on the bed, you can start to build up how long they stay on the bed. You can also build to pairing something that normally triggers your dog's Naughty But Nice behaviour, such as the doorbell ringing or the post arriving, with being a cue to Find That Boundary. The doorbell goes, your dog chooses the boundary and gets generously rewarded. Instead of rushing to nip the fingers of the postie when the letterbox opens, your dog will soon be rushing to find their boundary when they hear footsteps on the path.

Conversation starters

We love conversation starters! Conversation starters are a must-have tool for your toolkit: these are behaviours that are going to prompt your dog to engage with you. They are behaviours that your dog enjoys and can carry out easily in the face of challenges.

Our two favourite conversation starters are Figure of Eight and Two Up.

Figure of Eight

Figure of Eight is a fantastic game for simultaneously calming your dog down and bringing their focus onto you. To play, walk slowly with your dog, making a figure of eight as you walk. Walk slowly, calmly. At first your dog might strain against the slow speed, especially if their arousal level is up, but keep at it. If your dog is walking nicely, reward them. Occasionally stop. If your dog looks to you, reward them. Occasionally say your dog's name. If they turn towards you, reward them. If a distraction happens and your dog looks to you, reward them. Build that habit of calmness and engaging with you.

We recommend playing this game any time you arrive somewhere, for example, at the park, at the vet or at your training class. It is so good for calming your dog down after a journey and getting them in the right headspace for whatever they are doing next. And if you see a family in the distance in the park with a picnic? Engaging in a quick Figure of Eight will get your dog's attention back on to you and give you space to think, and that will put you back in control of how to approach the potentially tricky situation.

Two Up

Two Up – your dog placing their front paws on an object – looks like a cool party trick, but it has so many benefits for a Naughty But Nice dog. Dogs often find Two Up rewarding in itself, which makes it great to have in your toolkit if you find yourself short on food treats or if your treats aren't working. It is also a position of safety – if your dog has two paws firmly planted on something, they are not going anywhere.

To play Two Up, encourage your dog to place their front two paws onto an object. You can do this with equipment such as a foam balance pad, or household objects such as your bottom stair or a rolled-up towel. Use whatever you have to hand. Feed when they are in position. Pop it on cue once your dog has gotten to grips with it. Take it on tour and try it on natural objects like tree stumps and rocks. Get creative. Your dog will enjoy showing you what they can do!

You can also practise getting your dog to put Two Up on you. Some don't like to encourage their dogs to put their paws on them, and it may feel alien to some dogs at first. But if you have it on cue, then your dog should only do it if asked. Having the ability to get your dog to focus on you and in your body space can be a godsend in a Naughty But Nice situation.

Begin by sitting on the floor and encouraging your dog to stand on your thighs. You can lure if necessary. Then encourage them to place their paws on your chest. Add the cue. Rise to your knees and do it again. Then work to standing with your knees bent, then progress to standing fully upright. Where your dog will be able to place their paws obviously depends on their size. Keep it fun and keep it joyous – you want them to whip into that position when asked.

Turbocharge Two Up by really working on impulse control in the position. With your dog in Two Up, place some food on the ground beside them. Let them make the choice to leave the food. If they break position, cover the food. Let them choose to go back into position. If they don't, they lose the chance to get the food. If they do, give them the food. Make it even harder by dropping the food to the ground (just be ready to cover it where it lands should you need to – you'll need to be quick!)

Having your favourite conversation starters in your toolkit gives you confidence to know that you can manage your dog when things get tough. You'll always have a behaviour as a default to get your dog's attention back to you and that is so, so powerful in any challenging situation.

Honesty

Honesty is a very important tool in the Naughty But Nice toolkit. Don't be scared to be honest. It is a very difficult thing sometimes. But honesty is a crucial part of self-awareness, and self-awareness leads to learning and improvement. Don't kid yourself on just so you can stay comfortable. There are no real-life results in that. If you are not honest about what is happening, what you are feeling and what results you are getting, if something is going awry you won't be able to change it. So let's get your big honest pants on and meet our challenges head on.

Acceptance

Life rarely affords us the luxury of working on our issues in a vacuum. We can control our situations and manage our dogs as carefully as we can, but other people will still happen. Off-lead dogs will run up to you and your on-lead dog. People will reach out to pet your human-reactive dog. Children will run screaming past your fence. Accept that life happens.

Lack of awareness in others is a common problem for the Naughty But Nice dog owner. Just because we are working hard to understand what our dogs are trying to tell us doesn't mean that everyone else is. Sadly, many are not interested in what their dog is doing, never mind what is going on in your dog's head! Lauren has even been wee'd on by a dog whose owner was not paying attention!

When you are constantly bombarded by a world of unaware dog owners and humans in general – a world that appears to care not one jot for the issues you are working on with your dog – the best tool you can have in your toolkit to help you deal with it is to flip the feeling. Our instinctive reaction is to feel aggrieved and annoyed.

Lauren's story:

I was walking one day with my dogs, Brave and Style. Brave was off lead, but I had Style on harness and lead to prepare her for an upcoming agility competition. A huge black lab and a collie cross came flying around the corner and barrelled right into us. The owner appeared behind them. He was confrontational, ready to defend his unawareness of what his dogs were doing as they rampaged about. I could easily have lost my temper and gotten upset, but I consciously decided to ground myself and deal with it calmly. I flipped the feeling from angry to able. I changed my story from being a victim of the circumstances to being someone able to cope. I took some deep breaths, got my energy into a good place, engaged my dogs and got them out of there. I was able to walk away from the encounter without losing my cool.

These people will happen to you and you can't change them – just get your toolkit out and be ready for them.

Confidence

The number-one thing that can take a hit in a Naughty But Nice life is your confidence. It gets constantly bombarded and ground down by your experiences with your Naughty But Nice dog. Your dog feels your lack of confidence and it affects their ability to go about their business comfortably. They worry and look out for things that are scary – they can feel from you that something is off so they make it their job to look out for it, whatever it is!

Go forth knowing that you are armed with the tools you need to succeed. You've got this. You are ready and able to make the changes that will totally transform life for you and your Naughty But Nice dog.

Toolkit ready?

That Naughty But Nice toolkit is looking well provisioned already. Great! Now let's dig deeper into the concepts our Naughty But Nice dogs find most difficult. It is time to add the power tools.

CHAPTER 4

THE NAUGHTY BUT NICE DOG'S BRAIN: THE THREE KEY STEPS TO TRANSFORMING YOUR NAUGHTY BUT NICE DOG

Shaping your Naughty But Nice Dog's Brain

Your dog's brain is shaped by concepts, for example, optimism, grit, calmness, pessimism, nervousness and anxiety. All of the concepts in your dog's brain combine to produce the outcome: your dog's behaviour. Your dog's behaviour depends on what concepts are strongest and most well developed in your dog's brain. That means if the negative concepts are predominant or are your dog's strongest suit, then problems are going to occur.

Most trainers will typically focus on the outcome to try to correct it, i.e. the behaviour your dog is presenting with. But that doesn't solve the problem because the difficulties with the concepts in the dog's brain remain unchanged. The dog is no more equipped to deal with the problem than they were when the training began. To be effective, the training has to reshape the dog's brain. Your dog's brain is completely shapeable, and we do this through games.

The beauty of games-based concept training is that it is easy and fun. You can have literally zero dog training skills and still get real-life results. It is straightforward to understand and implement. You don't need to have scoured the scientific papers supporting the methods to play the games (unless you really want to!). It is simple: understand the concepts your dog needs to work on and play games that will work on them.

No one has to give you permission to train in this way. You don't need to be certified. You are good enough. In fact, you are more than good enough. No one else is more qualified or able than you to train your dog in this way. So get creative and get playing.

Getting started – get ditching!

The best place to start to work on your dog's Naughty But Nice issues is by ditching the routine and ditching the bowl. Every day, we start the day with a pot of value contained in our dog's food. And every day we typically throw away that value by placing all in a bowl in front of our dogs. When working on Naughty But Nice issues, training is going be happening all through the day, every day, so you are going to need plenty of valuable rewards. Don't waste your dog's daily calorie allowance by sticking it in a bowl!

Similarly, routines can be the root cause of many Naughty But Nice issues. Dogs are master predictors and the anxiety that comes with anticipation of certain events such as feeding and walking when they occur at the same time and in the same manner every day can lie at the heart of our dog's Naughty But Nice problems. Try where you can to mix things up so your dog is not always predicting what is coming next.

Mix Things Up

Laser target your training

The next step is to laser target your training. With Naughty But Nice dogs, it often feels like there is so much to work to do that it can feel totally overwhelming. Only 20% of what you do in training will get you 80% of your results. You only have so much food and you only have so much time in a day to train, so really hone in on the 20% of effort that will get you the results you need.

The three key steps to transforming your Naughty But Nice dog

Naughty But Nice behaviour manifests in many different ways, from biting, lunging and barking through to hiding and shutting down. But typically there is a common underlying cause. We usually find that three concepts require work in the Naughty But Nice dog: pessimism, inability to disengage, and an overflowing stress bucket.

The three key steps to transforming your Naughty But Nice dog are:

1. **Build optimism:** Naughty But Nice dogs are typically pessimists. They see they world as a scary place and interpret novelty as something to be very concerned about. They are unable to adapt to new situations and fear everything.

2. **Learning appropriate engagement/disengagement:** Naughty But Nice dogs struggle with engaging appropriately, either with their owner, other dogs or the environment, and disengaging appropriately. Such dogs will struggle to focus on their owner. They will also be unable to read other dogs' social cues. They will chase cyclists; they will be defensive or protective of their toys or food (resource guarding); they will suffer from separation anxiety.

Any attempt to encourage disengagement can result in a melt-down as the dog struggles to cope with the situation.

3. **Understanding and resolving bucket problems**: your dog's brain is a bucket that is constantly being filled by both positive and negative events. Naughty But Nice behaviour occurs when your dog's bucket overflows. Learning to manage your dog's bucket is absolutely essential to resolving Naughty But Nice issues.

Building these concepts is key to transforming your dog from one who reacts to everything to one who can easily cope with anything life brings their way.

And how do we do that? We play games! In the following chapters, we'll dive deeper into each of these concepts and the games that can help work on them.

Games-based training: will it work for my dog?

When you've lived with a Naughty But Nice dog, it can be hard to accept that something as simple as playing games can really work. You may have spent a lot of time and money in trying to resolve some really serious and potentially dangerous behaviours in your dog. You may have suffered multiple setbacks, made huge changes in lifestyle to accommodate your dog's behaviours and needs, and still found yourself walking the streets at midnight.

We understand. In a situation that seems so bleak, it can be hard to accept that games can really be that transformative. But they really can. They work for even the most serious of cases.

A real-life example

Nicola's story

Before I came to our Naughty But Nice camp at Devon Dogs, I thought there was something seriously wrong with my border terrier, Baxter. He was super reactive, to the extent that I had to walk him at odd times of day to avoid meeting any other dogs. He had bitten me and others. Things were really bleak and our relationship was at such a low point.

I was quite apprehensive about Tom the Vet Behaviourist seeing Baxter at the camp. No one wants to hear that their dog is broken, and that was what I suspected. But in three words, Tom transformed my whole relationship with Baxter.

"He's just scared", he said.

Tom explained that Baxter over processed everything and his pessimism was making him perceive almost everything as a threat. My whole outlook changed in that instant. Baxter was just frightened. Not broken. Not crazy. Just scared.

And the best bit was that there was plenty we could do about it. Games-based concept training has boosted Baxter's confidence, taught him to be optimistic and helped him to deal with whatever comes up. My confidence as Baxter's owner and teacher has skyrocketed. I know how to communicate with him now, how to teach him, how to help him get the best out of life. Our life together is fun now, thanks to games-based concept training.

Can games really make that much of a difference?

In a word, *yes!*

Games teach your dog:

- That novelty isn't scary
- How to deal with new things in the environment or new events occurring
- Problem-solving skills
- That different and challenging situations are fun
- To look on the bright side, transforming a pessimist to an optimist
- Confidence
- Self-control
- How to engage and disengage properly

They will also build your relationship with your dog. They will make your dog want to engage with you, rather than with the environment. Games also play a key role in helping manage your dog's stress bucket.

So let go of what has gone before and get playing!

A polite entreaty

On that note, it is important that we emphasise a key point. This book will only work if you do. Read and learn. Use the resources. Fill them in as you go. Then come back to them after you have worked on the concepts to see how you and your dog have improved. Play the games. Please don't just read: *do*!

CHAPTER 5

STEP 1: BUILDING AN OPTIMIST

Pessimism is the tendency for individuals to see something new or different or ambiguous as something negative or something to worry about. It is a typical tendency in a Naughty But Nice dog. We typically see the dog's behaviour and think that it is caused by a particular issue – for example, the dog doesn't like other dogs – but the root of the behaviour actually lies in pessimism.

Of all the behaviour cases Tom sees, 95% of them are looking for help with a specific problem, such as barking, fear of children or anxiety. The owner thinks that there is a specific issue going on, but all these difficulties stem from the same underlying general problem: the dog has a pessimistic outlook and anticipates something bad will happen, the dog is reverting to what they are bred for, and they have a chronically full stress bucket.

The purpose of pessimism

There are definitely benefits to being a pessimist. While the resultant behaviours of a pessimist outlook can be troublesome, the general concept of pessimism is an evolutionary winner. In survival terms, it is beneficial to be a pessimist. When pessimists hear rustling in the bushes, they do not go and investigate and consequently do not end up as dinner for the predator doing the rustling. They survive to breed and pass their genes on – including their tendency to be pessimistic; the optimists typically don't.

This is true of all species, not just humans. Dogs, cats, fish, birds, cows, even bumble bees win the game of life by playing it safe. Pessimism is effectively baked into the world's DNA. We've added to this by selectively breeding inherently pessimistic traits in certain breeds of dog as it benefits the work we want them to do. For example, a high tendency to notice novelty in the environment and other animals is a useful ability in a working sheep dog. However, the trouble comes with the modern life and the domestic situations most dogs now live in.

The tendency to pessimism that kept previous generations alive and able to do their jobs is not very helpful to a border collie living in a house in a city, trying desperately to cope with a life packed full of novel situations constantly bombarding its pessimist sensitivities. The very traits that brought the dog here are no longer necessary for survival or for their daily working life, but they are still deeply embedded and that leads to struggles.

These difficulties are compounded by the tendency of many to select their dogs based on looks rather than considering the purpose for which they were bred. Terriers are excellent examples of this. Small, portable, with spirited personalities and often incredibly cute, these dogs are a great choice for the modern family. But little does the family realise that they are born killers. The cute wee button chilling on their couch is ready to despatch creatures small and not so small, and yet they are often expected to be lap dogs. Their frustration that comes with not being able to express their genetic tendencies and functions is expressed through behaviour such as destructive chewing, pulling on lead, reactivity towards other dogs, escape artistry or failed recall.

That doesn't mean that certain breed types should be avoided. It simply means that rather than selecting dogs only for their appearance and size, we give some consideration to their breed purpose and think how to incorporate their genetic drives into their daily lives. By using a daily diet of games that tap into their breed drives, such as retrieve games for gun dog breeds and chase-and-catch games for terriers, and being careful to work on concepts such as topping up their optimism levels, there is no reason why you can't enjoy the company of your favourite breed.

The dark side of pessimism

Life as a pessimist isn't easy. It isn't a particularly happy life. Also, if your dog's pessimistic tendencies cause them to become stressed or results in stressful behaviours, it isn't good for their general well-being. Being chronically stressed is not good for any dog's body or mind, and can lead to ill health and even premature death, as the body struggles to cope under the constant bombardment of stress hormones.

What does a pessimist look like?

Of course, you have to work with the dog in front of you. So how can you tell if your dog is a pessimist?

THE PESSIMISTIC POOCH

Lauren's story:

I was working with Classic one day when I realised that something had gone wrong. She was behaving like a woman scorned. I couldn't work out what was going on with her. Three fields away, a whippet was whizzing in circles. Classic had spotted it.

Classic is a very able dog. She's a top-level agility dog, hard working and driven. But given a choice, her choice is often pessimism. And I can tell when she is feeling it! It is something we work hard on, always working to keep her optimism levels topped up.

Classic loves people. She is especially fond of children and gets to go to schools to listen to the children read to her. She just isn't happy with other dogs. I carefully manage her to try to avoid situations that will lead her down the pessimistic route. She generally expresses it subtly, but she is no more happy with other dogs than is a dog who is barking and lunging at the end of the lead. It is all about knowing your dog's signals, knowing how to guide them into a good outlook and knowing when they need an optimism top up.

Transforming the pessimist

So your dog is a pessimist. Is there is any hope? Are they destined to live life surrounded by a cloud of gloom?

Absolutely not.

Your dog's pessimistic outlook is something that is 100% changeable. You really can grow an optimist.

Lauren's story:

Tikki, my 12-year-old border collie, is noise phobic. She has always been a sensitive dog. She is retired now but she was a top-level agility dog, going to Olympia multiple times and also competing at Crufts. She won four Champ tickets. She's a hard-working, motivated, high-achieving dog. She is also a massive pessimist.

Any small noise around the house would set her off. Even something as small as a pen rolling off a desk and falling to the floor would send her into a corner, shaking and staring at the wall. I worked hard with her to help her turn around her perception of noise from something to be upset about to something that wasn't a big thing. We played games like Skittles and Noise Box to develop her ability to cope with noise novelty. I challenged her gently, in a way she could work through, to raise her optimism levels. I trained her in assistance work tasks: picking up keys, shutting doors, using anything that could make a noise. When fireworks season came around, I put music on and she learned to relax comfortably in her own space with a tasty filled Kong. I was always aware of her issues and considerate of her needs, and willing to adapt situations to make them work for her.

Sometimes it was hard. When a pessimist faces chal-lenge or a crisis, they will typically default to pessimism, and that can make it seem like you are making absolutely no headway at all. At times, I even doubted that I was the best owner for her. But I realise now that I am the best owner she could have.

> *I had to let go of the life I was 'supposed' to have with her – I had to give up that dream and embrace a bigger one. I had to let go of what I thought I was supposed to learn with her and go with what she was actually teaching me. I had to be courageous about what we could do together.*

Just because you find yourself in pessimist-land does not mean that it is not changeable! The resources available 12 years ago when Lauren first started working on Tikki's issues were very different to the help that is available today. Devon Dogs, absoluteDogs, Training Academy and Pro Dog Trainer all have resources to help address this struggle, which puts you light years ahead of where we were at back in the day!

We are in an exciting place of change. We are breaking down barriers, meeting the challenges head on and bringing the bright light of optimism to the world. Are you up for the challenge? Are you ready to bring your best, most optimistic self to the party? The world needs more optimists. Let's get transforming!

The hidden pessimist: being mindful

Pessimism doesn't always look like pessimism. Really look at the behaviours your dog is offering. Put your glasses on. Pay attention. Be mindful to what they are telling you. Daily life is so fast paced that we really tend to just take things at face value. But the language of dogs is so much more subtle and nuanced – we really need to open ourselves up to deeper consideration. Practising mindfulness can help with that.

THE PERSPECTIVE SHIFT

PICK UP ANY ITEM AROUND YOUR HOME
AND WRITE **10** THINGS ABOUT IT THAT
YOU HADN'T NOTICED BEFORE...

10 THINGS

THE ITEM

THE HUMAN TUNE-IN!

OVER THE NEXT 7 DAYS OBSERVE & NOTE WHAT **YOUR** DOG SPOTS / HEARS / SMELLS AND HOW THEY REACT

DAY	SEES, HEARS, SMELLS	REACTION
1		
2		
3		
4		
5		
6		
7		

DO YOU NOTICE A PATTERN?

The pessimistic dog's brain

Your dog's brain is made is made up of concepts. How skilled your dog is at any particular concept influences the choices they make in day-to-day life. All the concepts combined make up your dog's unique personality and determine your dog's ability to cope with whatever life throws at them.

If the concepts are predominantly positive, you tend to have a relaxed, happy, confident dog who is able to cope well with anything that arises. But if the concepts are mostly negative, you will have a dog who struggles with the demands of everyday living.

PESSIMIST BRAIN

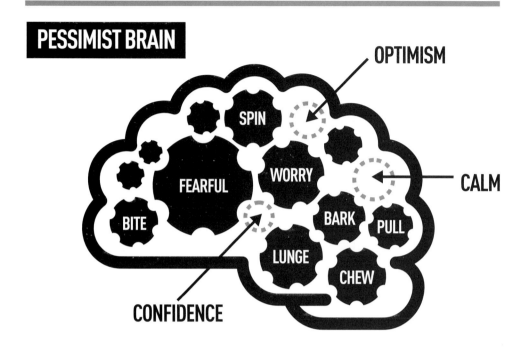

OPTIMIST BRAIN

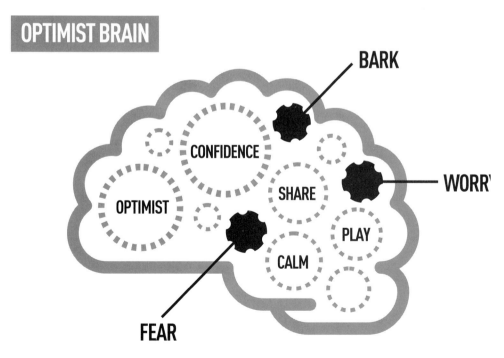

When your dog is in the pessimistic headspace, anything new, different or challenging will trigger feelings of fear and uncertainty. The deepest, oldest parts of your dog's brain don't like these feelings. The brain interprets them as a threat to survival and so *boom!* your dog is melting down at the end of the lead because a plastic bag blew across the path.

THE REACTIVE DOG'S BRAIN

STEP 1 - PESSIMIST TO OPTIMIST

PESSIMIST	**SCENARIO**	**OPTIMIST**
WHINE	KIDS BUILD A SNOWMAN ON YOUR	APPROACH
FREEZE	USUAL MORNING ROUTE	SNIFF
BARK		GREET & MOVE ON
LUNGE		
STACK		
AVOID		

STOP	YOU RELOCATE YOUR DOG'S	APPROACH FOOD
WHINE	FEEDING LOCATION TO	EAT NORMALLY
SLOW APPROACH	ANOTHER PLACE IN THE ROOM	
NOT EAT		

NEW LOCATION   NORMAL LOCATION

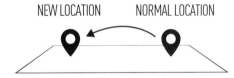

WORRY	NEW ADDITION	HAPPY
HIDE	TO YOUR HOUSEHOLD	RELAXED
BARK		APPROACH
GROWL		SNIFF
AVOID	OR	GREET
BITE		PLAY

Thankfully, a pessimistic outlook is something that is so, so change-able. You can teach your pessimistic dog to be an optimist through the power of games.

Transforming the pessimist: games for optimism

Here are two of our top games for building optimism: Noise Box and Reward Anything.

Noise Box

This is our favourite game for boosting your dog's optimism and remaining cool with novelty. Fill a box with items that crunch, rattle, move and shake, like empty bottles, cardboard packets or balls. Scatter your dog's breakfast in the box and let them hunt for it among the items. Use different types and sizes of treats to up the novelty even further and turbocharge the reward value.

As your dog hunts for the food, the items in the box will move around your dog's head. Your dog may also find the confidence to move them with their paws. Your dog will learn that things that move are not so scary and that staying cool gets great rewards!

Reward Anything

Nothing boosts a dog's confidence and optimism like the Reward Anything game.

To play the game, sit with your dog and reward anything they do, especially anything that is particularly bold, confident or inquisitive. It doesn't have to be big action – it could just be a small head move is a great place to start if your dog is particularly under-confident.

As your dog enjoys the rewards of their behaviour, their confidence will build and they will offer more and more. This game will make your dog feel like a hero.

Your own pessimism levels

You should also be aware that there might be two pessimists in your partnership. It pays to know if you are bringing pessimism to the party. If so, you can work to top up your own optimism.

> ### *Lauren's story:*
>
> *My first year with Tikki was horrible. I was overwhelmed by owning her. It was difficult as she was so emotional. My own emotions didn't help – I found it hard to let go of what I thought we 'should' be able to do together and that simply wasn't happening for us. I realised, however, that these thoughts just served to make the situation more difficult for all of us. I had to ground myself and adjust my thinking.*
>
> *I avoided putting myself in situations where Tikki and I would conflict, and I made sure I didn't actively participate in her emotional reactions. I really had to control myself and realise who had the bigger brain here. Agility was everything I wanted, but Tikki didn't want it – she found it stressful. Tikki didn't have a choice, I did – so it was up to me to make the best choice I could for her. She eventually went to the top of the game – we just took a different route to the one I had originally envisaged. And it was a route that taught me so much more than I could ever have imagined!*

Your attitude guides the course of the learning – your mindset determines the journey and course of the training. It all starts with you.

THE HUMAN OPTIMISM TEST

PESSIMIST

OPTIMIST

WHERE ON THE SCALE ARE YOU?

C

B

A

You are told a dog has to go to the vet to have his growth measured...

What do you think first?

A: The dog is a puppy and is going to see how tall he is

B: The vet is checking to see if the dog is overweight

C: The dog has a life threatening tumour and it is being measured
to see whether the tumour has grown

Transforming the pessimistic owner

And now you find out *you* are a pessimist. As if your Naughty But Nice journey hasn't been tough enough! An optimism boost is badly needed. What is a pessimistic owner to do?

Lauren's story:

My journey with Tikki taught me a lot about myself. It was a very emotional journey and very difficult at times. The major transformation happened for me when I found the deep, deep gratitude I had for everything Tikki brought to my life.

We had Tikki and her litter brother, Riot, from day one. Riot was a bright, happy, resilient, energy spring of a dog. You know if you call a dog Riot, you are going to have a party! He was an absolute dream, a real joy to be around. He was talented, fun, able, everything you could want in a dog. Tikki, with her negativity and pessimism and noise phobia, was such a different dog. Life with her was just less easy than with Riot. I hate to admit it, but I compared them. I saw Riot, how he behaved and the talents he showed, and I wondered why Tikki couldn't be like that. I couldn't just accept her and let her be.

Riot was killed in an accident at five years old. The moment he was killed redefined my relationship with Tikki. I realised how fast life is, and how something so perfect could be there then gone. Riot was my best friend. It hurt so much to lose him. My relationship with Tikki could have sunk even further, but instead it allowed me to appreciate what I did have. For all her ways, I was lucky to still have her. She was a living, breathing piece of him that remained with me, but she was also her own dog, with her own strengths, bringing her own cards to our relationship table. She stepped into the light and I woke up to what I'd been missing: the opportunities to learn, to help her, to work through her issues and achieve together. I saw the lessons that she was trying to teach me and I was ready to learn them.

GIVE GRATITUDE

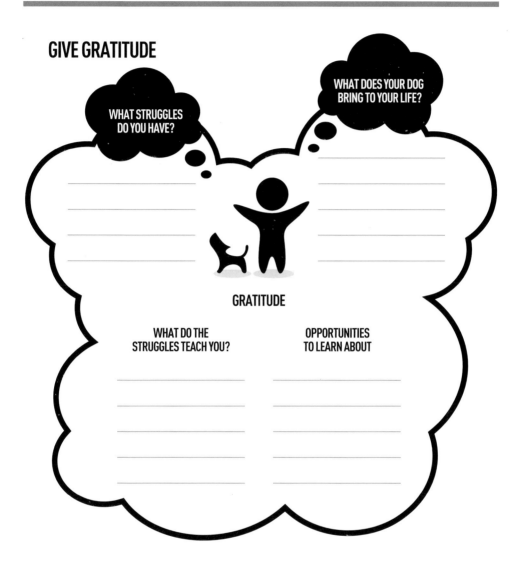

WHAT STRUGGLES
DO YOU HAVE?

WHAT DOES YOUR DOG
BRING TO YOUR LIFE?

GRATITUDE

WHAT DO THE
STRUGGLES TEACH YOU?

OPPORTUNITIES
TO LEARN ABOUT

Straightforward dogs are amazing. They are happy and relaxed. They are a joy to live with, to be around, to take out and about. Life is easy with them. You don't need to worry, to plan obsessively, to consider every option before you step out the front door. At absoluteDogs we have Abra, the nicest, most easy going Lab you could meet. She is wonderful. She has taught us to relax and live in the moment. She is the absoluteDogs Zen master. But the calm, gentle, easy going dogs don't teach you the tough stuff.

Some people aren't here for the tough lessons, and that is fine. The easy dogs are for them. But the tough teachings of the Naughty But Nice dog is likely to be your lesson – you are reading this book after all. You are in the right place. Hold tight to that and give thanks for it. Embrace it and own it. It is your journey.

The journey from pessimist to optimist

It is important to know and accept that there will be setbacks as you take your dog on the journey from pessimist to optimist, and as you yourself change. There will be setbacks, there will be difficulties, there will be doomsayers and naysayers. There will be those who just love to butt in without anything constructive to offer. There will be times when your dog defaults to old habits and you feel you have achieved nothing. Whatever the road throws at you, keep your chin up. Learn and move on. You are doing a great job. You are making a difference. This change will not happen – and stick – overnight, but it will happen. And your dog will be in a much, much better place because you took the time to understand this and to work on it with them.

Guarding your own optimism is huge. You are the driver of this change and you must be very careful to protect your own optimism.

If there is a person in your training class who constantly brings negativity, don't sit next to them. This person is coming for the optimism of everyone in the group. Beware! Always be aware of what other people and situations expose you to and don't be shy to stand up to protect your optimism. It isn't being rude. It is absolutely necessary for self-care and for the journey you are on.

Tell your dog how it is

A wise person once said, "your dog only knows how you say it is". If you say it is a great day, your dog doesn't know any different. Dogs live in the moment. So let your dog know that today is a good day. Set the tone. Encourage happy behaviours, like running, spinning or jumping, to let your dog feel great energy through movement. Clap your hands, give your dog a rub, chase them, dance with them, let them feel the joy. Play their favourite game with their favourite toy; give them their favourite food. Take a moment to sit with them and enjoy being together. Always look for ways to let them know that today is awesome.

WHAT DOES AN OPTIMISTIC DOG LOOK LIKE

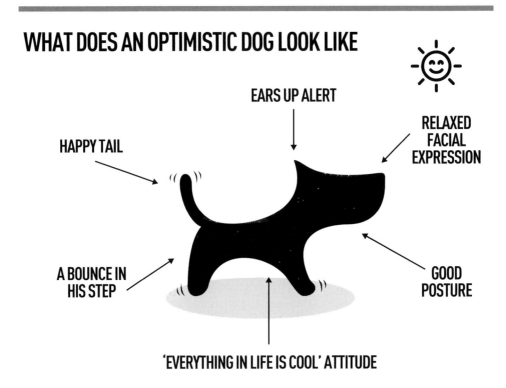

EARS UP ALERT

RELAXED FACIAL EXPRESSION

HAPPY TAIL

A BOUNCE IN HIS STEP

GOOD POSTURE

'EVERYTHING IN LIFE IS COOL' ATTITUDE

CHAPTER 6

STEP 2: LEARNING TO DISENGAGE

Learning to let go

Dogs with Naughty But Nice issues often have problems with disengagement. Disengagement is the concept of your dog seeing value in coming away from or leaving something they are interested in, engaged by or interacting with. It has many implications for everyday living. For example, if a dog sees value in coming away from the environment and coming when you call them, recall becomes a joy rather than a chore. Similarly for loose-lead walking: a dog who has trouble disengaging from the desire to get to the park will pull you the whole way there, but a dog who can put the thought to the side and find value in you will walk there nicely on a loose lead.

If your dog lacks the ability to disengage, their attention will readily become fixed on things. That leads to them being unable to disengage from objects, resources, people, dogs and situations. It turns your dog into an apparently wilfully disobedient, socially awkward nightmare.

Typical Naughty But Nice issues with disengagement include:

- **Separation anxiety:** the dog is not able to disengage from owner. When the owner is not available, this becomes a problem.

- **Difficulty with dog-to-dog interaction:** disengagement is important at every stage of interaction in the chain of events that happens when dogs meet and greet each other. If your dog has trouble disengaging, they will be unable to move from the front of the new dog to their rear end, which is what dogs will normally do. The other dog will know there is a problem and may react to that. Your dog may express their own frustration by reacting. Your dog's inability to disengage and tendency to give the other dog too much attention are a problem. The other dog will not appreciate the situation as the intensity of attention is uncomfortable for them. Your dog will also be unable to recall from the other dog.

- **Resource guarding:** the dog is unable to disengage from an item. It is important to note that dogs don't need to particularly like the item – it does not have to be their favourite toy or their food bowl. A dog can easily resource guard a random scrap of paper or a discarded tissue.

- **Pining:** a dog has trouble disengaging from the scent of a proximate bitch in season or coming into season will do anything to overcome anything that stands in their way. That can lead to your dog running out of an agility ring, or scaling your six-foot garden fence.

All of these struggles come from disengagement difficulty.

Lauren's story:

I was on the beach with my dogs when I encountered two border terriers with disengagement difficulties. The male was off lead, the female on lead. I was playing in the water with my dogs when they approached. The male dog followed us into the water. I took my dogs further into the water to increase the distance between us but the dog kept coming. His owner was calling him, but the dog was simply unable to disengage and kept coming.

The female dog was barking and lunging on the lead. The male continued to approach us. I asked the man to get his dog, but he replied that he didn't want to get wet! That is a broken situation.

STEP 2 - LEARN TO DISENGAGE

WHAT IS YOUR DOG'S DISENGAGEMENT ISSUE?

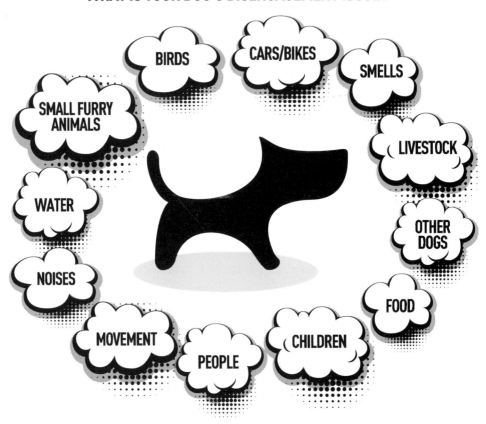

The bad news is that dogs who struggle with disengagement have stress buckets that tend to fill more quickly and take longer to empty. You can pass an ice cream lying on the ground on your walk to the park and when you arrive at the park 20 minutes later your dog will still be thinking of it when you unclip their leash, leading them to run straight back out the park and back to the ice cream.

Disengagement games

The trouble with disengagement difficulty is that it can often prompt an extreme reaction in your dog when you try to get them to disengage, from full on ignoring you to explosive screaming and lunging as you try to direct them away or biting if you try to remove the object. These reactions can be embarrassing if they happen in public, or even frightening. In all such circumstances, you know your dog is not in a good place mentally and that is upsetting.

The key to dealing with such situations is to have some disengagement tools in your Naughty But Nice toolkit. This will put you in a different headspace as you will have something to hand instantly that will help you deal with any situations that might arise. You will not be the owner standing mindlessly calling their dog's name over and over trying to get their attention as they bark and lunge at the end of the lead at the sight of another dog!

The Disengagement Game

This is our favourite game for Naughty But Nice dogs who struggle with disengagement. It is really easy to do, which makes it ideal for owners to practise at home and when out and about. It is simple for the dog to pick up, which also makes it great for puppies and rescues.

To play, you throw a piece of food towards something your dog is interested in (toy, tree, other dog, human). Let the dog go out to the piece of food and eat it. As the dog finishes eating, make a marker noise ('yes' or 'nice' work well) and as they look at you, walk away. As they join you walking away, feed them 20 or 30 times as you head in the opposite direction to the item of interest. In doing so, you place great value in coming away from the distraction.

To start with, play this game in the house. You can play it on a training line or lead outside if you are concerned that your dog may not be able to make the best choice to start with. Play with things that your dog is moderately interested in to start – don't go straight for the item that your dog will find hardest to disengage from. Build the skills first! Then you can take the game out and about, or try it on a more difficult object. Continue to develop it and you will soon have a dog who finds disengaging a privilege and not a bore!

A to B

This game is our favourite disengagement trigger. It is your dog's cue to disengage from something that is attracting their attention. As you walk towards whatever your dog is interested in, slide your hand down the lead towards your dog, turn around and walk away. As you do so, feed feed feed your dog.

The motion of your hand sliding down the lead is the trigger for your dog to disengage from what's ahead. You can include a verbal cue, but in situations when your dog is having trouble disengaging, a verbal cue is not likely to register with them. The motion of your hand sliding down the lead is a physical cue that your dog can react to instinctively, and it is thus more likely to prove effective in a sticky spot.

Building disengagement through games

How to disengage a puppy is a very important concept – yet at no point are we taught how. It is typically mentioned very briefly in recall training in Trainer Two type classes, when you are exhorted to "*be more interesting than the environment*". But just how do you achieve that? How can you teach a dog to disengage from something they find extremely appealing and give their attention to you?

The great news is that you can build disengagement in a young dog, a new dog or a dog who finds disengagement difficult. You can develop a dog who will choose to walk away from stimulation and will have a lifetime of good choices. If you work on disengagement in your training, you will soon find that the problems with disengagement in your dog's daily life become less of an issue and you will not need to bring the emergency disengagement tools out of your Naughty But Nice toolkit so frequently. You will transform your dog from an active coper, who deals with situations by acting out, into a passive coper, who deals with situations with calmness and can walk away without difficulty.

Food Prison

Food Prison is a fantastic game for working on disengagement. Set up a crate and put some tasty food in there. Lock that food up! Let your dog see the food and show interest in it. Wait for that moment when your dog disengages from the food prison and orients back to you. Mark that moment with a "yes" or "nice" and reward your dog. Then release them back to the food prison, open it up and give them the imprisoned tasty treat.

You can do this with food or a toy, or anything your dog really wants. Get creative. And always remember to be patient. Some dogs will persevere at this for quite some time before orienting back towards you. Allow them to make the choice – don't call them. You need them to be able to choose to disengage by themselves. You are building pathways in their brain for good choices so that the next time they encounter something that really interests them they automatically head for the great choice option.

Toy Switch

Toy Switch is a really fun disengagement game. Take two of your dog's favourite toys, and start playing with the one they find slightly less rewarding. Then let the first toy go limp and encourage them to switch to other toy. This should be their favourite toy, so switching should be a no brainer.

Continue to switch between the toys. If your dog struggles to re-engage with their second-choice toy, let the favourite toy go completely dead – let it fall to the floor and don't engage with it. Your dog will much prefer to play with the 'live' toy that you are waggling about and showing interest in. Again you are building those neural pathways that will making switching attention a breeze in a real-life situation.

The Mouse Game

The Mouse Game is an excellent disengagement game that you can play anywhere. (It also makes a really fun game to play for your dog's breakfast if you are ditching the bowl). All you need are a few pieces of food and your hand.

Place the pieces of food in a pile on the floor. Cage your hand over the food, spacing your fingers so your dog can see and smell the food but not reach it. Your dog will show interest in the food. They may try to access the food by licking, nibbling or pawing your hand. Don't let them get it!

Don't tell your dog to leave or give them any instructions. Allow them to decide to move away from the food. You are waiting for that split second when your dog takes their attention off your hand. That can mean they look away or they stop pawing or nibbling – just look for that moment when they stop actively trying to access the food. Some dogs will even make a very obvious move to back right off. Whatever form it takes for your dog, mark it with a "yes" or "nice", and then flick a piece of food from the pile out as a reward.

You can take this game on tour – if you can't place the food on the ground, hold it in your hand and cage your fingers around it. Play it in the garden, on walks, at the beach: get practising disengagement while you're out and about to get your dog making great choices in novel situations. Wherever you play, your dog will love it!

Improving your dog's disengagement skills

Working on boundaries is a great way to build disengagement skills. Boundary games build impulse control and encourage your dog to engage and disengage appropriately and to do so while working at distance, so they are building their skills and making great choices independently without you being right beside them.

You can add boundary fun to the Mouse Game. Pop your dog on a boundary (raised beds are great for this game) and place the food on the floor. You want to try to tempt your dog to leave the boundary to come towards the food. Your dog's job is to resist.

If your dog remains on the bed, take your hand off the food and slowly deliver bits of food to your dog on the bed.

If your dog leaves the bed, cover the food with your hand. Don't re-cue them back onto the bed. Let them choose to disengage from the food and return to the bed. As soon as they return to the bed, uncover the food and start once more to give them pieces of it.

Periodically, and as frequently as you need to in order to keep your dog excited and interested in the food, let your dog go directly to the food with a release cue.

Remember not to cue your dog to leave the food or to stay on the bed – let them make their own choices. Make it challenging for them in training: use extra-tasty, super-smelling treats and let them see them. Let them want them – the harder they find it to disengage, the bigger the win when they manage!

Engagement

While you work on disengagement, it is also important to work on appropriate engagement. Engagement can be a tricky one for owners to get their heads around, and it is something that owners often omit to actively develop. They can see that their dog obviously likes engaging with the environment but not so much with them. What's the deal with that? You feed them, walk them, play with them and love them, and they would still rather head off for a mooch than engage with you in the park! Your dog doesn't mean to punch you in the heart: you simply need to do a bit more work on engagement.

The majority of dogs come knowing how to engage with things. Pups are heavily engaged with their mothers. Most dogs will engage very readily with things, for example, toys, squirrels or other dogs. What needs work is your dog's engagement – or focus – on you.

How do we build engagement? Well, as always, there's a game for that! Or, in this case, all the games are for that! All games are engagement. Every game you play with your dog builds engagement and focus on you. And you and your dog have fun doing it, so it is a winwin all round!

What are you teaching your dog?

A game of tug is often used to encourage engagement in an otherwise tricky situation. For example, at an agility show when another dog is running, owners will often engage their dogs in a game of tug to avoid the dog barking during the run. In a bid to avoid their dog from becoming inappropriately engaged on the dog who is working, they will play like lunatics, with the owner gripping the toy and bouncing it madly, and the dog grabbing on and tugging with all its might. It might look like they are having a great game, but the energy about it just never feels quite right. It is all a little too manic.

When you use a tugger in such circumstances, you really need to think about the energy you are creating (hyped up, wired) and where this is focused (on the tug). What are you teaching your dog? The dog is not really engaging with you. They are engaging with the toy. All their energy, focus and frustration is directed into the toy. That's not a great energy to be work with. It is unlikely your dog would be able to disengage from the tug toy in that situation if asked to do a simple known behaviour such as sit, which is a sign that their arousal level is way too high.

Always be aware of what you are teaching your dog. Instead of teaching the frantic direction of energy onto a tug toy, think:

- How can I lower my dog's arousal in this situation? How can I calmly shift my dog's focus from the dog who is running to me?

- What food games can I use? Food games have a much better energy in these situations. The energy in food games is a lot lower and calmer than toy rewards.

- Do I need to create more space to make disengagement from the working dog and engagement with me happen? If so, using A to B to get out of there to somewhere a bit quieter will give your dog the head space they need to make great choices.

We are quick to use food games now at events, rather than a toy. We feel it gets a better quality of work and interest from the dog. It keeps the dog's brain in a better place and gives a much better energy. And if we see that our dogs' brains are simply not in a place for learning, and we are just managing their reactions, we will get them out of there. There is no point persisting in that situation. Your dog will not learn anything. Their brain just isn't in a learning place. Get them out of there.

You see a lot of owners persisting in such situations, trying desperately to manage the situation with a tugger, or yanking on the lead and calling the dog's name over and over as the dog barks and lunges. Such situations can be embarrassing and people just want a quick solution that will stop the behaviour. The owner feels bad and doesn't know what to do. It is a situation common to the Naughty But Nice owner and it feels horrible.

These situations stem from a lack of understanding. Everyone wants to do their very best but sometimes we just don't know what the right thing is and don't have the necessary skills to effect the change we are looking for. It is easy to shove a tug into the dog's mouth or to physically drag them away.

But there are better solutions. We as owners can make better choices for our dogs. Arm yourselves with the tools you need to manage those situations, and train for the situation at home in your daily training by working on appropriate engagement and disengagement. You will find that you have everything you need to help your dog engage and disengage like a pro.

Our go-to games for engagement

Scatter Feeding

Scatter Feeding is wonderful for stopping inappropriate engagement because it breaks the dog's eye contact with whatever is catching their attention. If your dog is staring at something, be it a squirrel, cyclist or another dog, for longer than three seconds, there is a good chance they have lost the ability to disengage and they are going to have a struggle with good choice making.

Scatter food on the ground near you to get your dog's focus back on to you. Let them see you dropping the food to bring yourself into their field of attention. You are where the fun is at now!

Middle

Getting your dog into the middle position automatically puts their focus back on to you as they have to physically work with you. It is also a position in which many dogs feel really secure, which can help them to disengage from something that is troubling them. Also, some dogs find the position itself incredibly rewarding and will readily engage to fly into that spot between your feet with joy.

To teach Middle, stand with your feet apart and use a tasty piece of food to lure your dog into the space between your feet. Feed them in that position. Break them out of the position by throwing a piece of food out, then lure them back in with another piece of food. Again, feed feed feed in position. Your dog will soon find the value in that spot.

Do be aware, however, that Middle is not necessarily appropriate for every dog. Some dogs may need a lot of encouragement to enter your body space in that way, and some dogs will find it too much to have you standing over them. If your dog is not keen, never force them – simply choose another game that they do love.

Magic Hand

Magic Hand is such fun. It is brilliant for snapping your dog's attention onto you, and also for guiding your dog out of a sticky spot. Your dog will be too busy waiting for you to make the next piece of food appear to bother about what's going on elsewhere in the environment.

To play Magic Hand, have a supply of small pieces of food in your hand. Hold your hand above your dog's head, palm upwards, just slightly forward so the food will fall to their face. Allow a piece of food to fall from between your fingers for your dog to catch. When your dog has finished eating and looks back up to your hand, drop the next piece.

Keep it fun

Variety is important when encouraging engagement. Keep mixing it up so your dog doesn't know what is coming next – that is how you stay interesting! Also, don't nag your dog to engage with you. It is important to let them make their own choice. That is what is going to stand you in good stead when you find yourself in a tricky situation. You have to maintain the element of letting them make their own (great!) decision.

Engagement and disengagement: the key tool to a dog who can cope with life

Knowing when and how to engage and disengage appropriately is essential to your dog being able to function properly in the world. Difficulties with engagement and disengagement lie at the heart of so many Naughty But Nice issues. Unfortunately, that understanding is not typically taught at training classes and, when it is covered, the focus is often directed solely towards engagement without also teaching disengagement. Both are so, so necessary!

Our Pro Dog Trainer and Training Academy students are taught the value of appropriate engagement and disengagement from day one. It can be so damaging if done badly, because your dog will establish mental pathways for making inappropriate choices that become a learned behaviour and create a blueprint for future situations. That will take a massive amount of work to undo. Teaching and establishing appropriate engagement and disengagement are vital from the outset.

CHAPTER 7

STEP 3: UNDERSTANDING AND RESOLVING BUCKET PROBLEMS

Introducing the bucket

The bucket represents your dog's brain. Your dog is constantly exposed to things that can pour into their bucket – these things can be positive (like your dog doing something they really enjoy) or negative (like your dog being exposed to something they find worrying or don't know how to deal with).

When your dog's bucket is full, they can't think straight. Everything spills out, and then we have problems. And you just never know when or where that bucket is going to overflow. You don't know what experience is going to be the last drop that causes your dog's bucket to overflow.

What does a full bucket look like?

- Barking or being more vocal and lunging
- Struggling to settle in the house
- Pulling on the lead
- Jumping up
- Being distracted or struggling to focus on you

- Irritability (with you, your children, other dogs or pets in the household)

- Hiding away or avoidance

Within virtually all Naughty But Nice dogs, you will find a massively overflowing bucket.

This is not a training issue

These are not behaviour problems: they are dog behaviour. They are simply your dog's way of expressing that all is not well in their world and they are not able to cope with a particular situation. And these behaviours are a good indictor that your dog's bucket is full.

Any attempt to train in a moment when your dog's bucket is full or overflowing is doomed to failure. Your dog is just not in a mental place to be able to actively learn.

It may also appear there is no rhyme or reason to when your dog exhibits Naughty But Nice behaviour, but this is not random reactivity. It is an accumulation of events – which can be either positive or negative – that have been ongoing. Your dog has just now reached their tipping point.

STEP 3 - BUCKET PROBLEMS

WHAT CAN FILL A DOG'S BUCKET?

POSITIVE

EXCITEMENT
ACTIVITIES
HIGH ENERGY PLAY
GAMES
DO-ING

NEGATIVE

WORRY
FRUSTRATION
FEAR
ANXIETY
PAIN
ITCHINESS
GASTRO-INTESTINAL
UPSET

So many things are piling up in your dog's bucket, many of which we are unaware of or don't even consider. We don't even realise they are going in there – for example, dogs barking in the next van when we park at a show, or expecting our dog to work all day at a training workshop without any adequate breaks. How often have we mistaken an overflowing bucket for lack of motivation? With a Naughty But Nice dog, it is an oversight than can lead to real problems.

Improving your dog's bucket

THE BUCKET... THE 4 ELEMENTS

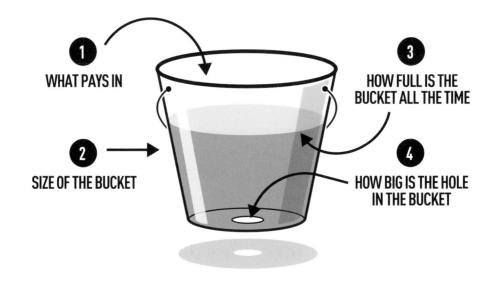

1 WHAT PAYS IN

2 SIZE OF THE BUCKET

3 HOW FULL IS THE BUCKET ALL THE TIME

4 HOW BIG IS THE HOLE IN THE BUCKET

ILLUSTRATE YOUR DOG'S BUCKET

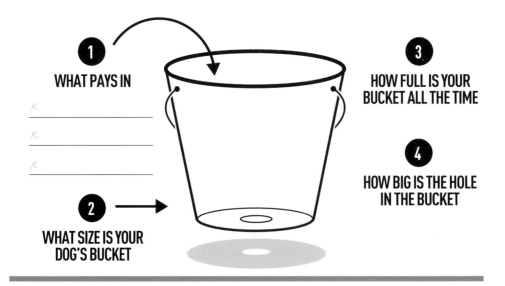

1 WHAT PAYS IN

2 WHAT SIZE IS YOUR DOG'S BUCKET

3 HOW FULL IS YOUR BUCKET ALL THE TIME

4 HOW BIG IS THE HOLE IN THE BUCKET

The key to improving your dog's bucket is understanding how it works. There are four key points to the bucket:

1. **What goes into the bucket:** this can vary. It can be positive experiences such as meeting a favourite dog friend, visiting a much-loved family member, chewing on a tasty bone, going for a walk or spending time with you. Or it can be a negative experience such as being left home alone, a random knock at the door or hearing a loud bang.

2. **The size of bucket:** this influences how much exposure to events your dog can tolerate before their bucket overflows. It is important to note that the size of a dog's bucket does not correlate to the size of the dog – you get Chihuahuas with massive buckets and Great Danes with miniscule ones.

3. **The size of the hole in bottom of the bucket:** this determines how quickly the bucket empties.

4. **The average daily fill level:** this determines how full is bucket all the time – does the dog live in calmness or not in calmness? Your dog's lifestyle and daily living experiences will determine the average level of the contents in their bucket at any moment.

The great news is you absolutely can – and should – work on each element of the bucket. Each element can be expanded or improved. If you work on what is filling your dog's bucket, the size of their bucket, the size of the hole at the bottom of the bucket and managing the average fullness of your dog's bucket, their bucket will overflow far less frequently. You will be well on your way to extinguishing your dog's Naughty But Nice issues.

How do we do that? There's a game for that, of course!

Bucket-boosting games

Novelty

The concept of novelty is a useful one to work on for managing what goes into your dog's bucket. A negative reaction to novelty contributes a lot to the bucket, whereas a dog who is cool with novelty will carry far less in their bucket.

Ball-Swamp Breakfast

Get a cardboard box and fill it with light items that your dog can easily move around, such as ball-swamp balls or empty plastic bottles and scrunched up pieces of paper (use anything you have to hand that is clean and safe). Sprinkle pieces of your dog's food in the box too, and allow your dog to hunt for their meal. This game is amazing for building confidence, as your dog gets lots of wins very easily while coping with the novelty of the items in the box moving round their face. You can turbocharge their motivation by using a variety of tasty treats – kibble mixed with cheese and hot dog sausage, and in different-sized pieces, so your dog never knows what they are going to get next. That again shows them that novelty is a great thing.

Scatter Feeding in Novel Places

This is an awesome game to build your dog's confidence with novelty while out and about. Use some of your dog's daily food allowance to have a fun game of scatter feeding in a novel place. Find a nice spot, sprinkle your dog's food into the grass and let them hunt. Your dog will soon pair new locations with having fun!

Arousal

Can your dog perform a well-known behaviour such as sit or down when they're excited? To improve the size of your dog's bucket, you want to get them listening and thinking in arousal.

Working on bringing your dog's arousal up or down can increase the size of the hole in the bottom of your dog's bucket, too.

Thinking in arousal is a major focus of the Naughty But Nice programme and the Training Academy, where we have a wide array of games that will greatly expand your dog's bucket.

Simon Says

Grab your dog's favourite toy and have a play together. Break off playing and ask for a behaviour they know well. Start easy with a short period of low-intensity play and ask for a behaviour they know super well. Then make it more challenging by upping the intensity of the play and asking for a more difficult behaviour.

Arousal Up, Arousal Down

This is a simple game that gets great results. Bring your dog's arousal level up by playing with a toy, then have them calmly lie down and be fed. Again, keep the intensity level low to start with, then build it up.

Levelling off

Working on the average daily fill level of your dog's bucket requires less of a game and more of a strategy. Be very aware of your dog's life and what is filling up their bucket at all times. Seek to manage it actively. You can't avoid everything that is going to go into that bucket, but you can recognise and understand when your dog has been exposed to a lot and then choose to give them more chill time.

For example, if you know you have a big agility show coming up at the weekend, try to lower your dog's average bucket level in advance by giving them some chilled-out days before the event. Or if you know your grandchildren are visiting in the afternoon and your dog is going to be running round mad with them, let the dog have some relaxation time with a tasty chew in the morning. Be aware of what is coming up in your dog's schedule and plan accordingly.

Working around the bucket

We need to work on expanding the size of the bucket and the size of the hole, and managing what is going into the bucket – but while that is happening, we need to meet the dog half way. Don't put your dog in a tricky situation that is inappropriate for its bucket. We can control the dog's bucket by controlling what we expose the dog to.

Tom's story:

I was dealing with a behaviour case in which the dog didn't like the owner's child. The dog had been labelled dangerous and aggressive. In truth, the dog simply just had a very small bucket.

The baby was loud, novel and strange. When the baby started moving and crawling, the dog's behaviour worsened. A moving, unpredictable being is a very scary prospect when you are a pessimist with a very small bucket. It goes against a dog's instincts to be aggressive towards a human so if a dog is getting to the stage they are biting, they are under such a high level of stress that they are probably experiencing more pain than any bite. That, however, is of no succour to a mother faced with the prospect of a dog who apparently hates and wants to harm her baby!

We dealt with the situation by limiting the dog's exposure to the baby. The dog was simply not near the baby. The dog was also given plenty of opportunity to be taken away from the situation to empty their bucket. At the same time, we worked to increase the size of the hole in the dog's bucket through playing games.

It was not the individual relationship between dog and baby that was the problem. The dog did not hate the baby. The dog's bucket was too small to cope with the baby. Babies are novelty machines and the dog just couldn't cope with what had happened to their world.

A tale like this is much like the stories we tell ourselves about our own dogs or the labels that are put on them: he's aggressive, she's a biter, he bolts, she's timid – the dog will stay that way unless and until we change their story. We tell ourselves that the dog has malicious intent but that isn't true: the dog's brain just isn't suitable for the situation you've put that dog in. Their bucket is just inadequate.

Not just one bucket

Another essential in bucket management is appreciating that you are dealing with two buckets. You too have a bucket. And it works in just the same way your dog's does. You also need time after a stressful event to unwind, and you too will find your average daily fill line rises if you have a succession of stressful days. You too will end up exploding if your bucket overflows. Take some time to think about what fills your bucket and how you could manage that to stay well under spilling point.

THE HUMAN STRESS BUCKET

WHAT FILLS YOUR STRESS BUCKET?

POSITIVE	NEGATIVE
NEW JOB	LOSE JOB
PARTY	ILLNESS
EXERCISE	WORK ISSUES
FAMILY VISIT	CAR BREAKS DOWN

POSITIVE **NEGATIVE**

100%

0%

STRESS BUCKET

100%

0%

STRESS BUCKET

Consider your own self-care. Sometimes a walk is not what your dog needs that day: sometimes a walk is not what *you* need that day. Living with a Naughty But Nice dog is very emotionally charged. Be aware of your own energy and always take it into account when working with your dog.

ENERGY BALANCE

ENERGY UP

_____

_____

_____

_____

_____

ENERGY DOWN

_____

_____

_____

_____

_____

Of course, our energy levels are changeable. Know what brings your energy up and down, and tuck some energy changes into your own toolkit for an instant energy boost or calm should the need arise.

Quick human energy boosters:

- Have a sugary snack or drink

- Listen to your favourite high-energy song

- Clap your hands

- Get moving: jog on the spot, do some jumping jacks, anything that gets the blood pumping

- Listen to a motivational speaker, podcast or audiobook

For quick calming:

- Take a few deep breaths

- Go for a walk

- Get a massage

- Stroke your dog

- Have a handkerchief to hand with your favourite calming scent – lavender is fabulously calming

How do you know what is going into your dog's bucket?

The best way to manage bucket problems is to be mindful of what is filling up your dog's bucket. Really get to know your dog: pay attention to every little thing, positive or negative, that excites or worries them. What do they love or hate? Listen to what they are trying to tell you.

Watch for signs of your dog's bucket being fuller than normal. The key is to become an expert observer of your dog. Know what works for your dog. Know what your dog's positive and negative stressors are. Notice what has an impact on them. Notice what is normal for them physically, psychologically, emotionally and behaviourally, and recognise and identify any changes in the norm. Take action on any changes by giving your dog a few days of rest and relaxation.

Bear in mind that Naughty But Nice dogs tend to be over-processors. There are things that go into their buckets that other dogs would not even notice. We humans can be the same.

STEP 3 - OVER PROCESSORS

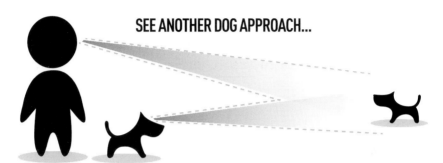

SEE ANOTHER DOG APPROACH...

OPTIMIST

OH HEY

HI

HOW ARE YOU?

WANNA PLAY?

SEE YA LATER...

DOG OVER PROCESSING

I'M WORRIED

I NEED TO GET AWAY

I DON'T KNOW WHAT TO DO

HELP ME!

HUMAN OVER PROCESSING

OMG! HERE'S TROUBLE

HE MIGHT ATTACK MY DOG

HOW IRRESPONSIBLE

I DON'T KNOW WHAT TO DO...HELP!

When you appreciate how busy the world is to a Naughty But Nice dog and how much they are letting in, you begin to realise why their buckets are always so full. Our Naughty But Nice dogs are regularly having huge dumps of negative stress into their buckets (which tend to be small to start with) – no wonder they overflow so quickly!

It is important that we be aware of what our dogs are trying to tell us. They are talking to us all the time, but we tend not to listen. Most people are just not aware of what their dog is trying to tell them. They don't catch the big things, never mind the small things – and that is pretty scary. Big things can include a curled lip or a growl, or the dog backing away with their tail tucked between their legs, or even biting.

Before the dog escalates to that stage, though, they typically exhibit smaller behaviours such as a flick of the eye, side eye, a shift in balance away from a stressor, a worried expression, tail carriage (is the dog's tail held high or is the hair on it fluffed out?) or stiffness in their stance. These are all clues that the dog is not comfortable. If we pick up on those clues, then the dog will not have to move on to the bigger, more difficult or dangerous behaviours.

Use your senses to really tune into your dog and really get what they are trying to tell you. If you do, they won't have to shout so loudly!

HOW DOES YOUR DOG TELL YOU THEY'RE NOT HAPPY?

BEHAVIOUR

BODY LANGUAGE

Naughty But Nice dogs will also often have common triggers, events or occurrences that pay so much into their buckets that overflow is guaranteed. For example, Lauren's dog Fiji gets super excited by the agility ring, so she doesn't get near the ring until it is time to work. She is managed away from the ring. Be aware of your dog's triggers and have some ready-to-roll solutions primed in your Naughty But Nice toolkit for those potentially challenging moments.

SITUATIONS WHERE NAUGHTY BUT NICE BEHAVIOUR SHOWS...

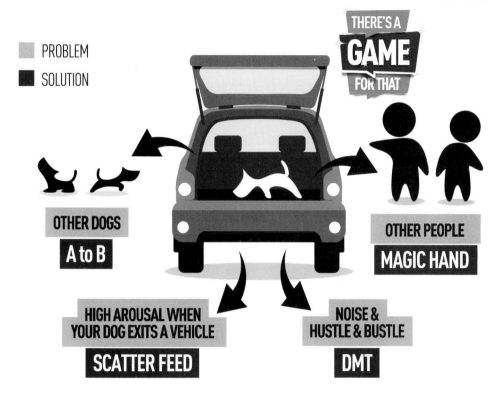

PROBLEM
SOLUTION

THERE'S A **GAME** FOR THAT

OTHER DOGS
A to B

OTHER PEOPLE
MAGIC HAND

HIGH AROUSAL WHEN YOUR DOG EXITS A VEHICLE
SCATTER FEED

NOISE & HUSTLE & BUSTLE
DMT

Give your dog a break

What do you do if your dog is letting you know that their bucket is rapidly filling, or if you realise that they've had a really busy time of it and need to let their bucket empty? You give them a break.

What does a break look like? It depends on the circumstances you are in at the time and what is right for your dog (dogs all enjoy different ways of relaxing, just like humans). Your dog might find chewing calming – if so, filled Kongs, bones and chews are great and easy to take out and about for a ready-to-implement relaxation option. Having a portable zone of comfort such as a covered crate or place in your vehicle where your dog can chill out is perfect for managing your dog's bucket at events. Scent can also be calming for dogs – a quick game of scatter feeding, while active, can actually be calming when that bucket level is rising.

Be your dog's expert and guardian

You are your dog's expert, guide and guardian. We hate to break it to you but you are going to have to get bolshie about your Naughty But Nice dog's bucket. All too often, we struggle in silence with our dog's issues, embarrassed by how they are behaving or not wanting to ask for help. No more! As your dog's bucket manager, it is up to you to let others know what your dog needs.

> ### *Lauren's story:*
>
> *Active bucket management is something that is super important to me. I have a dog with a small bucket that fills very quickly and overflows spectacularly. For that reason I have a strict no-petting-the-dog policy for visitors. That rule is there for a reason. It keeps both my dog and my visitors safe. I don't feel uncomfortable about making the rule known and reinforcing the message if necessary. I'd rather be firm with my visitors than leave it to my dog to tell them!*

Tips on how to get family and friends on board with your dog's needs

- Explain why your dog has these particular needs and how the rule benefits your dog and the humans they interact with.

- Make it as simple and easy as you can to follow and implement the rule.

- Have consequences if they do not follow the rule (ones that you, rather than your dog, enforce) – for example, if your parents will not walk your dog on a lead, then they can't take your dog out, or if a family member refuses to knock so you can get your Naughty But Nice dog into their safe space before they enter, lock the door.

- Have a can-do attitude. Negativity is unfortunately all too common, and people can be very resistant to anything that is unusual or requires them to change. Be upbeat, see the rule as positive and as something that will help your dog get along happily as part of the family and be safely part of the experience.

mes it's a matter of people just having to get on with it – they just have to get on board with what you and your dog need. If they can't, it is up to you to make the call on how you interact with them when your dog is involved and how you manage the situation. It is not wrong to take account of your dog's needs, no matter how many invitations you have to turn down.

A major pain in the daily life of the Naughty But Nice dog owner is the Unaware Other Dog Owner. We've all met them. They are the one that lets their off-lead pup run up to greet your on-lead Naughty But Nice dog, with a call of *"it is ok, he's friendly!"* Those are truly words no Naughty But Nice dog owner wants to hear.

In that situation, we henceforth give you permission to be as blunt as you need to be to convey the message that that situation is not ok for you and your dog. A firm, *"fine, but my dog is not going to enjoy the experience"* should suffice. But if it does not, do not hesitate to repeat the request firmly until the Unaware Other gets the picture. It is not rude to ask someone to call their dog away if their approach is going to cause you or your dog distress.

The ultimate investment

Keeping an eye on your dog's bucket has massive benefits. Your dog will be happier, calmer and better able to participate in and enjoy daily life.

So pay attention to your dog's bucket. Know what fills it up. Keep it as empty as possible. Work to expand it and to help your dog to empty it quicker. In doing so, you will find that many of your Naughty But Nice challenges are simply no longer a thing.

CHAPTER 8

TRANSFORMATION: THE POWER OF GAMES

It might not feel like it, but Naughty But Nice issues really can be blessings in disguise. They are often the catalyst for change you need in your dog training and daily living experience with your dog.

Sometimes a dog comes to you because it was meant to change your life. So often we spend so much time resisting our Naughty But Nice dogs and trying to 'fix' them that we can't see them for what they are: a beautiful opportunity to learn and grow. We get it: it is hard to find the positive when your dog is putting holes in the postie. But your dog's Naughty But Nice issues really do present an amazing opportunity to get under the hood of your dog's behaviour, to experiment and to see what can resolve the issues, in a fun and positive way. Your confidence will grow as you see real-life results, and your bond with your dog will deepen as you work through your dog's Naughty but Nice issues together.

Don't stay stuck in the problem

When you have a Naughty But Nice dog, it can be easy to get stuck in the problem. Life can be tough as a Naughty But Nice owner, and you can find yourself in some truly awful situations. It is in our human nature to dwell on these, to talk about them to try and work them out, to worry and wallow in the problem as we try to get our head around it. It is a common thing – the world is addicted to its problems. But all it does is keep you firmly centred in the problem. And that is no way to live.

Previously you may have believed that your Naughty But Nice dog was exhibiting problem behaviours. Now you know that it is just dog behaviour, and that when they are reacting or acting out or being clingy, they are just trying to tell you something. You know that your dog is pessimistic, unable to engage and disengage appropriately, and is struggling with a small bucket that fills easily and quickly and empties slowly. The previous training you've tried hasn't worked because other types of training don't alter these things.

It is time to leave the past behind. Leave the disappointment and upset, the sadness, the loneliness, the frustration – let all that fall away. Let your problems become opportunities, your struggles become strengths.

Don't stay problem based. Embrace the Gamechanger way. Become solution based. It is a beautiful way to live. If we all spent more time working on the solution to our problems, rather than chatting about them, how many more problems would we solve and how much more quickly could we turn our problems around? The solution-driven life is a much better place to be. It makes for a far more pleasant and productive life. So shoot for spending 5% of your time on the problem, and 95% of your time on the solution.

Change your story

The Gamechanger way finds simple and fun solutions to difficult situations. The first step is to change your story. Don't labour under labels. Naughty But Nice is a handy label to help others quickly understand that your dog has certain needs, but it is not a label we ever want to see anyone hide behind or use as an excuse for not fulfilling their dog's potential.

There are Naughty But Nice dogs out there all over the world enjoying walks in busy parks, recalling on busy beaches, living in multi-dog households, coexisting with cats, participating at the top level in dog sports – it is all so, so possible. You just have to change your story. Yes, your dog has Naughty But Nice issues, but you are working on those and your dog is going to grow beyond them to write the next chapter in their life book with you. And what that chapter will be is up to you to dream. You and your dog can do anything.

The power of games

Playing games is the ultimate solution. The power of games is immense. Problem solving can traditionally feel like something heavy, something to be ploughed through and undertaken only because the pain of staying where you are is more than the pain of trying to change. But games change that. They are transformative not just for our dogs, but for us too. They encourage us to develop the same flexibility that we want to see in our dogs. They grow us into better trainers and make us more fun for our dogs to work with. They top up our optimism levels and help us rediscover a lightness that can all too often get lost in a life with a Naughty But Nice dog. They give us the power to be a bigger, brighter, better version of ourselves and to bring something truly awesome to our dog training. And you thought it was just your dog's life we were changing!

Games make a big difference to dogs, humans, families, relationships and lives. They work on every level, at all stages of life and in every situation. They are life changing. You can change anything with a game. You can change everything with a game. Games allow the opportunity to change, to get creative, to grow, to improve, to achieve. There is so much power in them. They open the doors to so many things: there is literally no limit to what can be achieved through games. They make anything possible. They are the best super power ever!

What's next?

We want to take a second to reiterate how lucky your dog is to have you. You care enough to read this book and to seek learning that can change your dog's life. Your dog could not have a better owner.

But –

And this is a big but –

You do still have work to do.

Reading and learning alone are not going to help your dog. It is time to get to work on those concepts that will help your dog and to work through the three steps in this book, playing the games and completing the resources to help you fully implement all you have learned.

And then...

You must keep learning.

Learning and doing, learning and doing, learning and doing – that is how we improve. Always seek to add new tools to your toolkit. To get to the dream that formed the heart of your powerful why, you need to keep skilling up.

If you keep going over the same information or keep playing the same games, your results will flat line. You must always keep learning! Visit www.absolute-dogs.com where you will find a wealth of blog posts, books, and DVDs to completely immerse you in Gamechanger learning. Always, always keep learning. That is the key to continued real-life results.

THE RESULTS PLATEAU

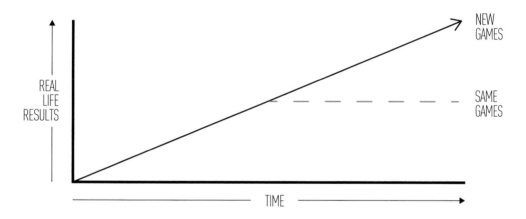

Taking it further

Want to boost your learning to continue getting real-life results? With a wealth of games to explore and fresh new games hitting your inbox each week, the absoluteDogs Training Academy is the place to be to take your games-based learning to the next level. Want to be first to hear when the Academy next opens? Sign up here: https://absolute-dogs.com/pages/training-academy.

Are you a trainer seeking to transform the lives of the Naughty But Nice dogs and owners in your classes? The absoluteDogs Pro Dog Trainer Programme contains everything you need to know to guide the Naughty But Nice dogs in your care: from dealing with the first owner contact, through setting up your training room for maximum support, to how to structure your sessions to get the best out of your Naughty But Nice dogs and humans. Sign up here for a shout-out when enrolment for the next Pro Dog Trainer programme opens: https://absolute-dogs.com/pages/pro-dog-trainer.

Dream. Do. Achieve. Live your very best #naughtybutnicelife

CHAPTER 9

BONUS CHAPTER: SUPPORTING YOUR NAUGHTY BUT NICE DOG'S TRANSFORMATION

You get out what you put in

Like your dog's brain, what you put into your dog's body has a direct effect on what you get out in terms of behaviour, energy and general wellbeing. From pets to top level sports dogs, it is important to be aware of what you are putting into your dog. This is especially true for the Naughty But Nice dog. Always feed the best quality food you can afford and use the best quality treats. Just as you would for your own food, keep an eye on the ingredients, look for the purest ingredients possible.

A delicate balance

Naughty But Nice struggles can often have their roots in the complex interaction between your dog's brain health, gut health, and training. Training is usually the go-to fix for any struggle, but if you fail to appreciate the role the dog's brain and gut health play in the mix, then there will be significant road blocks in your path to success.

Your dog's brain

As for humans, levels of brain chemicals such as serotonin influence your dog's mood, calmness, energy levels, and the choices they make. Low levels can lead to depression, anxiety and aggression. Like humans, the levels of brain chemicals occurring in your dog's brain, and how your dog's brain processes these, varies naturally.

Your dog's gut health

Our dog's digestive system is not something most of us give much consideration to unless they have, 1. eaten something they shouldn't, or 2. something is manifestly amiss. But your dog's gut and their brain are closely linked. They interact and that interaction can have profound implications for your dog's behaviour, with imbalances leading to stress related conditions such as a lack of calmness, and fear and anxiety.

Also, the community of tiny microbes that live inside your dog's gut, the microbiome, directly creates neurotransmitters like serotonin, as well as influencing production in other body areas, in turn directly impacting brain health.

Keeping everything in balance

It is therefore vital to keep your dog's brain and gut health in balance. A good quality, varied, healthy diet plays a key part in this and is the foundation upon which your training efforts rests.

Our interest in the interplay between diet, behaviour and training led to us developing our own supplement: Calm-K9. We use it as part of a multi-targeted approach to resolving Naughty But Nice issues:

1. Re-shape the dog's brain via games.

2. Make sure the brain has everything it needs to perform at its best and re-shape in the best, most efficient and most effective way.

3. Make sure that the dog has a healthy gut.

Our Calm-K9 supplement supports your dog's brain and gut to make sure that your games based concept training is as effective as it possibly can be and gets outstanding real life results.

The ingredients of champions

Calm-K9 contains five top ingredients for brain and gut health:

1. Tryptophan

2. Passiflora incarnate

3. Lemon balm

4. L-glutamic acid

5. Enterococcus faecium

Tryptophan

Tryptophan is an essential amino acid for all mammals. It cannot be made by the body and has to be supplied by diet. Tryptophan helps to make niacin, melatonin and serotonin. Serotonin is a mood stabiliser and helps with sleeping, eating and digesting. It also helps regulate anxiety, happiness and mood. Low serotonin levels can lead to issues such as depression and anxiety in humans, and have been linked to increased behaviour associated with aggression in dogs and other animals.

Tryptophan has to compete with other amino acids to be transported to the brain. If you increase the levels of tryptophan available, you increase the chance of it being carried to your dog's brain, where it will influence serotonin levels. Current evidence suggests that the concentration of tryptophan transported to the brain influence the levels of serotonin produced.

Passiflora incarnate

Passiflora extracts have long been used traditionally to treat a range of anxiety based behaviours. Passiflora is believed to increase concentration of the neurotransmitter GABA (Gamma-aminobutyric acid). GABA combats brain over-activity and reduces anxiety. It also has a calming effect on the nervous system, promoting calmness and sleep, and boosting mood.

Lemon balm

Lemon balm has an anti-anxiety effect. The active ingredient in lemon balm stops the breakdown of GABA thus increasing the levels of GABA in the body. GABA combats brain over activity and reduces anxiety. It also has a calming effect on the nervous system.

L-glutamic acid

L-glutamic acid is converted to GABA in the body. There is evidence to suggest that during times of psychological stress, lower amounts of GABA are produced in the body. Treatments for anxiety in humans target the GABA system.

Enterococcus faecium

Enterococcus faecium is a probiotic that promotes gut health. The gut has been implicated in a variety of stress-related conditions, such as anxiety and depression. Gut microbes can directly stimulate nerves and send signals to the brain, and gut microbes can produce neurotransmitters that are identical to those produced by the body.

Gut microbiota are important in metabolising tryptophan in order for the body to make serotonin.

The benefits of Calm-K9

The Calm-K9 ingredients work together to help to reduce anxiety, calm the brain, stabilise mood, promote feelings of relaxation, happiness and pleasure, stimulate motivation, and enhance the reward system. Calm-K9 also helps to promote gut health, thus ensuring that your dog's gut and brain work together in harmony. Calm-K9 supports your dog from the inside as you work to reshape their brain through games-based concept training. Now that's a super powerful combination!